Maxime Vivas

Not so Zen

The hidden face of the Dalai Lama

Max Milo

ISBN : 978-2-31501-106-3
Max Milo Editions
Collection Essais-Documents, Paris, 2023
www.maxmilo.com

Not so Zen
The hidden face of the Dalai Lama

To Frédéric, for his precious help

"The political regime of Tibet before the Chinese invasion was sometimes described by Western observers, when they discovered it in the 19th century, as a "feudal theocracy". This traditional society was characterized, in fact, by political and economic structures reminiscent of those that existed in Europe in the Middle Ages, and in particular by a union of temporal and spiritual powers.[1]

"Outside the monasteries, our social system was subject to a feudal regime. There was a total inequality of wealth between the landed aristocracy and the poorest peasants."[2]

"[...] under the impulse of our religion, we [...] will bring forth a new Tibet as happy in a modern world as it once was in its isolation."[3]

---

1. Report of the Franco-Tibetan friendship group of the Senate, June 14, 2006.
2. Dalai Lama, *Memoirs of the Dalai Lama. My land and my people*, Paris, John Didier, 1963.
3. *Ibid.*

Preamble

The harsh and lofty land of monasteries, where everything was serenity, love of neighbor, spirituality and harmony, has been impoverished, deprived of its culture, martyred by a genocidal colonial power (the Dalai Lama has sometimes used the word *holocaust*). Such, in short, is the image of Tibet, so widespread that anyone who dares to draw a different one, or even to nuance it, exposes himself to a backhanded collage of infamous labels.

I was in Tibet in July 2010 for the news website *Le Grand Soir* (legrandsoir.info) with a group of journalists (*Le Figaro, Le Monde* and two freelance reporters). At first, I wasn't sure my companions would see the same thing I did. What's the point of traveling," said Seneca, "if you take yourself with you? True, but hadn't we slipped into our luggage a piece of who we are and a part of the medium in which we express ourselves? When we read what each of us wrote on our return, we will see that this was the case, but without excess. Objective facts were brought to the attention of the respective readerships, which did not prevent, also (but not instead), the addition of an opinion, that is to say of the subjective.Of course, everyone is free to let his or her pen run wild about the nature of the central power in Beijing, to draw on his or her archives to evoke Tibet's past, to extrapolate about its desirable or desired future. But after noticing, for example, that store signs, street names, street signs, and newspapers are written in Tibetan (and then in Mandarin), after seeing the existence of Tibetan-language radio and television stations, after visiting a university where students and their professors have developed software in Tibetan, no one could support the antiphon of cultural genocide. And none did. It would indeed be more credible to write that, at home, regional cultures would like to be bullied in this way, Tibetans benefiting moreover from a compulsory teaching of their language in schools from the first classes and in the first cycle of secondary school (teaching in Mandarin and English in the second cycle).

In short, beyond our differences, which we can only welcome in that they demonstrate that France is not a country of unique thought, there remains a "common trunk" of things seen together at the same time and which are the truth, even if they had never been written by the Dalai Lama's lauders nor by the media where journalists read each other and practice what Pierre Bourdieu called "the circular circulation of information".

Friend," the old backpacker will whisper to Candide, "don't forget to say that everything is not at its best in Tibet and that the system in place cannot please a Frenchman. We do indeed have some good provisions in our Constitution that would be useful in Lhasa, the capital of Tibet, and in Dharamsala, the Indian capital of the Dalai Lama's exile (and I am not thinking only of the strict separation of Church and State and the ostentatious occupation of public space by one belief, and one belief only).

The race to modernize Tibet, the increases in the standard of living, the subsidies to the economic sectors, the construction of schools and hospitals, the development of solar energy, the preservation of nature, the conservation of sacred texts, the development of culture the respect of customs, the restoration of monasteries, the free practice of Buddhism in temples and in the street, none of the journalists (whose opinions cover a wide political field) with whom I traveled wrote a line to say that this is pure communist propaganda. Their criticism was directed elsewhere.

So I'll talk about things that we've seen together that I'd be surprised if any of my four colleagues, beyond our different approaches, would claim that they were the product of my partisan imagination.

The reader will have noted this luxury of introductory precautions. In France, it is fashionable to talk about the past of the Catholic Church, about the Pope's past, including his (forced?) as a teenager in a Germany under Nazi rule, on the irruption of Islam in our fantasies since the attack of September 11, 2001 in New York, on Judaism which was persecuted in Europe and in the name of which Palestine is being broken and crumbled, But woe betide anyone who does the same on the taboo subject of Tibet and on the fourteenth Dalai Lama, idol of the media and winner of the Nobel Peace Prize, as untouchable as Mahatma Gandhi, Abbé Pierre, Nelson Mandela or Martin Luther King, to whom his zealots wrongly compare him.

What place are you talking about, asked the Greek sages? They were inviting us to look at the interests and motivations of our interlocutors. I therefore sought to find out who the Dalai Lama and his most fervent supporters are in France and in other countries.

During a debate in a Toulouse bookstore, I heard an old Spaniard warn: "Whoever speaks up does so in order to hitch others to his wagons." And to add mischievously: "I myself, at this moment..." The warning applies to this book. Yet in most of the following pages, the floor will be given to the Dalai Lama himself and to others who are sympathetic to him, including lovers of Tibet and Buddhism. I will also refer to reports following study trips by French parliamentarians of the left and the right which qualify or contradict the Dalai Lama's propaganda in France on many points.

When critical opinions or information will be brought by others (parsimoniously), cross-checks will have been carried out beforehand and the sources will be quoted to allow the reader to verify them. We cannot, in fact, give up all of a sudden on giving voice to the voices that, just about everywhere in the world, have torn off the mystifying mask of the Dalai Lama, nor even to the point of view of the Chinese authorities, nor to the work of their statisticians, economists, demographers, historians, who will not be insulted by claiming that nothing they say is in conformity with the truth, especially when they put forward facts that are verified elsewhere and that are attested to by international organizations and researchers of all countries.

I
The untouchable

There are indeed two faces of the Dalai Lama. The first is a permanent smile, a sign of kindness, wisdom, tolerance, pacifism and inexhaustible patience in the face of persecution. It is the one on the covers of magazines and countless books devoted to Tibet in France and in many other countries.

The second frowns, those of a fallen monarch whose life is devoted to a supreme goal: to return to Lhasa to restore a theocratic power which, even if it could not be restored to its former state, would not differ in essence from that which he once enjoyed, a power which he had inherited from his terrible predecessors and which he did not hasten to reform in order to eradicate an unheard-of institutional violence which the civilized world had banished for centuries.

France has a high rate of unemployment, precariousness is growing, families are breaking up, many French people live in fear of the future, companies are faced with a series of suicides, and we are the leading consumers of antidepressants in the world.

At the same time, we are witnessing a decline in the first religion of France. Churches are emptying. In the countryside, there is often one priest for several parishes. People marry less, they confess less, they are stingy with the collection of money for the church. Crisis of faith, criticism of the Vatican's recommendations, rejection of the

Pope's infallibility, increasing doubt about the dogmas that facilitated evangelization. The devil with cloven feet has disappeared from preaching, God is no longer sitting on a cloud, the story of Eve's birth by amputation of Adam is perhaps a bad translation of the texts, etc. Paradise is less and less well defined, the promise of the survival of the soul by frequenting places of worship has lost its attractive power.

Almost every hour, the media give us news of a new god before whom everyone is invited to bend the knee in the electronically equipped temples called "stock exchanges" and where modern saints with barbaric names are pampered: "CAC 40", "Dow Jones", "Nasdaq"...

However, materialism has never been sufficient to fill a human life. A variable part of spirituality, of dream if you like, of hope of a benevolent impalpable, exists in each of us.

And the transfer takes place. The belief which declines here, undermined by a history of the Church devoted to the rich, the powerful and the armies, guilty of a thousand crimes, one goes to seek it elsewhere, in a religion for us immaculate, with new rites, adorned with the virtues of the peaceful love of its neighbor, able to dispense an unhoped-for interior calm, even to preserve health, carrying deliciously exotic words, perfumed with yak butter candles, sheltering in its monasteries, where multitudes of priests display themselves in saffron robes, gigantic Buddhas shining under the gold leaf, a religion of which Mecca is the "Roof of the World", a religion symbolized by an eternal public smile plastered *urbi et orbi* on the face of a living and itinerant icon, a kind of international Care Bear for grown-ups. Thus seen, the Buddhism of the Dalai Lama is able to seduce not only the Parisian bobos and the babas cool (even if they were the first to become active proselytes), but other layers of the population in search of spirituality, happiness, or simply discovery. And why not?

The problem is that, behind the possible intrinsic virtues of Buddhism, there are masters of thought of flesh and blood, of appetites and ambitions, of nostalgia for a lost power and of an era (of stagnant unhappiness) that they magnify, as we will see in a moment.

Buddhism: I wrote *religion*. Is it not rather, in the absence of a revealed god, creator of the universe, a philosophy, a spirituality? The polemic can swell from the only answer to this question. The Dalai Lama, living proof of the immortality of the soul, who is reborn, not from anyone (and he proves capable of demonstrating this at the age of four), but from a Dalai Lama, is therefore entitled to call himself the spiritual and temporal head of an immense territory whose inhabitants are his flock. They call him His Holiness, prostrate themselves before him as others do before the Pope, venerate the effigies of his predecessors (his is forbidden in China) and the Buddhas in temples where candles burn in front of altars. Monasteries, a liturgy, monks, a cult, sacred texts, songs, devotional gestures, prayer wheels, prayer flags, the promise of an afterlife. It looks like a religion. Complete with a philosophy, with tools for "working on oneself"? If you like. Let's avoid a quarrel on this point, because this is not my purpose here. But having noted that the Dalai Lama himself writes *religion*, I will stick to the word, without underestimating what it may be reductive for the reader who is looking for (and who may find) something else in Buddhism.

However, if Buddhism is only one philosophy, it is the only one today in the world which is dressed in such finery, obliges to so many rites and whose great master intends to direct in his name an immense territory from which would be banished all the other philosophies and even his own followers who pretend to deviate one iota.

Before continuing, let it be clear to everyone that neither the relevance of a cult nor that of the Chinese political system will be discussed in these pages. Many others have written about this, and I have chosen to deal with another subject: the Dalai Lama, spiritual master of a few hundred million Buddhists in the world, but appearing, through the power of the media, as the only pope and aspiring to become the all-powerful leader of a territory as big as five times the size of France, occupying a quarter of the territory of

China, and where all law derives from the dharma (the universal law of Buddhism), that is to say, from the religious texts.

The question is to know what would be a "free Tibet" led by a prophet not necessarily well informed about the horrors of Nazism, who dislikes science[4], in mourning for a high country over which he reigned and whose anachronisms he is not yet able to recognize.

The question is also whether democracy would benefit in China and whether the world would be better off for it.

The question is finally to determine whether the media-humanitarian agitation around Tibet is not a simple attempt to replay in China the "Orange Revolution" like the one that, remotely controlled and financed from abroad, shook Ukraine in 2004 to serve the geopolitical interests of the American empire.

We will try to answer these questions, at the end of a rational analysis based essentially, I repeat, on irrefutable texts, almost all of which are borrowed from the Dalai Lama, his affidés or from indulgent observers.

---

4. See Chapter III.

II
A Dalai Lama bogeyman

"Respected throughout the world, received by heads of state, the man in the saffron tunic and communicative laughter continues to embody the hopes of six million Tibetans living in Tibet or in exile," said an AFP dispatch dated November 22, 2008.

The television channel France 24, which broadcasts international news and wants to be a "French CNN", is more doubtful about the Dalai Lama's debonair authority over the whole of Chinese Buddhism. On August 9, 2009, the program *Reporters*, its news magazine, broadcast a report by Capucine Henry and Nicolas Haque.

And what we saw there with horror, it is a dalaï-lama pronouncing on January 7, 2008 "a speech of a rare violence in a university of the south of India" (dixit France 24), a dalaï-lama Father Fouettard enjoignant to his faithful in exile with him not to speak with their brothers and sisters, followers of Shougdèn.

Shugden is a deity of the Buddhist tradition, worshipped all over the world, in China, India, Nepal, Mongolia, Bhutan, Bengal and even in Russia, Europe and the United States.

Already on August 12, 2005, in a public speech in Zurich, the Dalai Lama had declared his hostility to a belief that no longer pleased him: "Some of you may know, but others may not, that in the Tibetan tradition there is the practice of a deity called Dorje Shugden, that some people follow this practice and are followers of the veneration of this deity, and that I have declared myself against this practice because it goes against my principles and those of the Dalai Lamas. "

France 24 reports on the process of making a decision in which the exiled sage "strongly condemned the Shugden movement and its followers". Admirers of the self-proclaimed world spokesman of a gentle and Zen democracy, opposed to the Chinese political system, will listen with dismay to His Autocratic Holiness: "I did not ban the Shugden for my own interest, I have carefully meditated and thought about it in my soul and conscience."[5]

The blacklisting is followed by concrete effects: His Holiness's followers condemn their brothers and sisters to the street, and they are now victims of serious discrimination in their daily lives. Posters warn them of the places where they can no longer enter. A Tibetan man testifies that in his village in South India, all doors are closed to him and to the members of his community. In a few months, these deviants have been banished from a community reputed to be fraternal, since it is Buddhist. And France 24 asserts: "The Shugden monks can no longer enter shops, public places and even hospitals. In the streets, one can see the portraits of their leaders plastered on the walls, like outlaws."

Ah, let's beware of these easy comparisons that provide a pretext for decrying an entire argument. However, the prohibition for a designated minority to enter stores, the posters with pictures of the enemies "and our brothers though"...

What is worse is that the Dalai Lama practiced this cult before advising against it, banning it, and then pillorying those who remain faithful to it and who, for this reason, are designated by him as agents of Beijing, an accusation that makes them fall into the rank of pariahs in a country, India, where the Dalai Lama does not, however, officially write the law. Should we anticipate the fate that would be reserved for the Shugden in a Tibet of which he and his

5. France 24, quoted broadcast.

followers would be the masters? Can we anticipate the worldwide outcry that such measures taken in Tibet by the Beijing government would provoke against the branch of Buddhism of which the Dalai Lama is the head?

The excommunication having been pronounced, the propaganda only has to justify it. And if the Dalai Lama has decided alone, his followers must enter the dance of demonization. In Dharamsala, a village in the Himalayan foothills of India where the "Tibetan government in exile" is based, the Prime Minister explains that "the Shugden are above all political enemies, enemies from within. One of them, very influential, is guilty of a serious act: he "visited China at least two or three times". The tone is set: "They are ready to kill anyone, to hit anyone," he says. The Shugden are therefore assassins, but above all traitors in the pay of the Chinese, according to those close to the Dalai Lama. The Shugden and the Chinese are linked, that's obvious," continues [the Prime Minister]. Shugden practitioners are all financed by the Chinese.[6]

The accusation, unsubstantiated, does not lack salt coming from people close to a Dalai Lama who has been financed for decades without much discretion by the CIA[7].

In 2003, Kelsang Gyaltsen, the fourteenth Dalai Lama's envoy to the European Union, stated that the Dalai Lama was in favor of separation of church and state and that he had made a decision not to hold any position in the Tibetan administration upon his return to Tibet. This might be welcomed by all if his current decisions did not demonstrate that the methods of government in Tibet under his rule and that of his predecessors continue to guide his meditative unconscious in India.

We see here a double discourse since, in the context of his trip in August 2011 to the south of France, to Toulouse, the Dalai Lama had an information document published where, in the paragraph

6. *Ibid.*
7. See Chapter X.

entitled *The Promotion of Harmony between Religions*, we read these excellent things: "As a Buddhist monk, and a practicing religious man, the Dalai Lama also has as his objective the promotion of harmony between all religious traditions. All the world's religions are based on ethical values of compassion, love and tolerance. Because human beings have diverse aspirations and dispositions, it is important and necessary to have different religions in our world. At the basis of a harmonious relationship between different traditions, there must be mutual respect, understanding and esteem."[8]

That's all there is to it. It remains not to do in its fiefdom, black eye, finger pointed and high verb, the opposite of what one whispers outside by supporting a bow, the joined hands and a malicious smile lighting the face.

Far from being "respected throughout the world", the Dalai Lama, who represents one out of four branches of Buddhism in Tibet (the "Yellow Bonnets"), two percent of Buddhists in the world, is now contested, even by some of those who have followed him into exile. Disdainful (as we shall read) of the other fifty-five ethnic groups that make up China, he can only legitimately claim the almost unanimous support of the major Western media, which, by warming up and (de)shaping public opinion, incite demagogic politicians to bow down to him with devotion.

This devotion never goes so far as to follow the Dalai Lama in his demand for Tibetan independence. All the member countries of the UN (where China does not only have friends and supporters of its rising power) recognize that Tibet is a Chinese region and not a nation occupied by another. In January 2011, while receiving Chinese President Hu Jintao in Washington, Barack Obama reaffirmed that "the United States recognizes Tibet as part of the People's Republic of China. In other words, not a single country follows the Dalai Lama in calling for Tibetan independence. None of them advocate putting the idea to a vote in that region. The

8. http://www.dalailama-toulouse2011.fr/FR/ssdl_engagements.php

Constitution of France, which is "one and indivisible", does not provide for the possibility of a regional or national referendum as a prelude to the break-up of the country. We would therefore be ill-advised to encourage it elsewhere.

Under these conditions, why should we wish a partition of China for the benefit of a man whose amnesia the French, who have forgotten nothing of the Second World War, will find strange as soon as it comes to Nazism? On September 10, 2006, Georges-André Morin, a freethinker, told France Culture: "It is amazing to note that the current Dalai Lama, in 1994, wanted to bring together in London Western personalities who had known an independent Tibet. Of the seven personalities, there were the two Waffen SS, Harrer, the mountaineer, and Beger, the Auschwitz ethnologist, and a Chilean diplomat by the name of Miguel Sorano who made a career in the wake of Kurt Waldheim, being close to Pinochet and the Nazi communities of southern Chile." In April 1999, the Dalai Lama appealed to the British government to release Augusto Pinochet, who was arrested during a visit to England.

In the daily newspaper *Libération*, Laurent Dispot returned to the subject, writing that Heinrich Harrer had joined the SA in 1933, as soon as Hitler took power, that he passed to the SS and that he was "a favorite of Reichsführer Heinrich Himmler. "He was given a mission by Hitler and Himmler himself: to infiltrate Tibet, in agreement with the regent ministers of the Dalai Lama as a child, in order to become his tutor.[9] The supporters of "Harrer the mountaineer" argue that, having been absent from Europe during the Second World War, he did not participate in the atrocities committed by the SS. This is true. He only carried out a mission "with mystical, racist and strategic motives" in a search for the pure races. He spent the rest of his life trying to hide his Nazi past, preferring to rave about a Tibet in which he saw the "typical example of clerical dictatorship".

9. Dispot (Laurent), "Le dalaï-lama et l'honneur nazi", *Libération*, 25 April 2008.

The Dalai Lama erased this episode of his childhood. To read it, the noise of the second world war collided with the thickness of the walls of the monastery-palace of Potala. At most, he learned about "episodes". "But at home, we were not concerned with external events.[10] So SS Harrer never talked about it? In any case, the wise man never distanced himself from this very special tutor who had come on a mission on the orders of the Führer. On the contrary, he never stopped thanking him for having been his "initiator to the West and modernity"[11].

The relationship between the Japanese guru of the Aum sect, Shoko Asahara, sponsor of the "Tibetan cause", and the Dalai Lama is also troubling (photos show them hand in hand). However, Shoko Asahara made the horror headlines by gassing passengers in the Tokyo subway with sarin on March 20, 1995.

Finally, as we shall see, his relationship with the CIA is troubling.

It is therefore regrettable that, in his struggle for independence, the Dalai Lama has little regard for the choice of his methods and his allies, friends and financiers.

---

10. Dalai Lama, *op. cit.,* p. 50.
11. Dispot (Laurent), *op. cit.*

III
The still reign

Lhamo Dhondrub was born in the village of Takster at an altitude of two thousand seven hundred meters, in the province of Amdo, on July 6, 1935. The village would later become Hongya and Qinghai province.

At the age of two, the child provides "proof" that he is the reincarnation of the thirteenth Dalai Lama. Rationalist minds may express their skepticism, but that is not the purpose of this book, so no further comment will be made. In the same way, let his mother assure us that the child, whose mother tongue was the Chinese dialect of Xining, spoke spontaneously at the age of two in Lhasa Tibetan, the language of his predecessor. The Dalai Lama himself takes care not to confirm this too incredible legend.

Lhamo Dhondrub is decreed the fourteenth Dalai Lama under the name of "Jetsun Jamphel Ngawang Lobsang Yeshe Tenzin Gyatso", which can be translated as "Holy Lord, Sweet Glory, Compassionate, Defender of the Faith, Ocean of Wisdom". But he also does not dislike being called "Yeshe Norbu" ("Accomplished Jewel").

He began his monastic education at the age of six. At the age of fifteen, in 1950, he acceded to power by anticipation by being enthroned spiritual and temporal leader of Tibet.

Between 1950 and 1959 (when he fled to India), the Dalai Lama thus reigned for nine years, accommodating himself, his regent and his advisors in practices where religious freedom, women's freedom (in the case of adultery, women's noses were slit and their ears cut off), peasants' freedom, in short, freedom and compassion for the people, were no more (or less, no doubt) accepted than in medieval France. In his *memoirs*, he explains that he was preparing to carry out reforms just as the Chinese army entered Tibet. His culpable slowness left it to the central government in Beijing to abolish slavery and serfdom, to abolish corveys and private religious justice, to create schools, to make the people literate, to revive a demography that had been stagnant for two centuries and to almost double the life expectancy of citizens.

Slavery has been outlawed by the Geneva Convention since 1926, by the International Labor Organization (ILO) since 1930, and by the Universal Declaration of Human Rights since 1948 in its Article 4: "No one shall be held in slavery or servitude; slavery and the slave trade shall be prohibited in all their forms."

The fourteenth dalaï-lama, last of a long line in power, takes flight in India on March 17, 1959. On March 28, eleven days later, serfdom and slavery were abolished in Tibet (neighboring countries where monks did not rule had done the same, much earlier: 1923 in Afghanistan, 1956 in Bhutan). The measure benefits almost one million Tibetans, that is to say ninety-five percent of the population, those who did not belong to the castes of aristocrats, monks, living Buddhas: the masters.

The harshness of monk rule in the Tibet of the Dalai Lamas is such that it seems appropriate not to talk about it and, when others expose its abuses, to quibble over words. For example, there is a controversy about the reality of slavery and serfdom. Let us refer to the definition adopted in 1956 as a supplement to the Geneva Convention of 1926, and more precisely to the "Supplementary Convention on the Abolition of Slavery, the Slave Trade, and Institutions and Practices Similar to Slavery". It defines serfdom as follows:

"Serfdom, that is, the condition of any person who is required by law, custom, or agreement, to live and work on land belonging to another person, and to render to that other person, for remuneration or free of charge, certain specified services, without being able to change his condition."

Did the miserable Tibetans escape these constraints? The Dalai Lama himself, in his *Memoirs, is* careful not to assert this, on the contrary. As for slavery, the convention defines it as "the state or condition of an individual over whom any or all of the attributes of the right of ownership are exercised.

Alexandra David-Néel was a great traveler, friend and undisputed specialist of Tibet. She had been received in Dharamsala by the Dalai Lama and, after her death, he visited her native house in Digne, in the Alpes-de-Haute-Provence, on two occasions (October 1982 and May 1986). He publicly paid tribute to him for having made known the Tibetan culture to the Westerners. In her book *Great Tibet and Vast China,* she concedes: "A kind of benign slavery still exists in many parts of Tibet.[12] The Dalai Lama's relentless denial of this reality quibbles with some of the freedoms granted to the poor, which do not constitute slavery.

The laws of the Dalai Lamas of Tibet bear striking similarities to a French text of 1685, *L'Édit du roi touchant la police des îles de l'Amérique françoise,* known as the "Code Noir", by Colbert, which officially aimed to provide legal protection for slaves. In the royalist France of yesteryear and in the theocratic Tibet of yesteryear, masters had the right to punish their people, to force them to practice a religion, to punish runaways and thieves, to have them chained, whipped, imprisoned, amputated, to put them to death, to grant or not to grant permission to marry. As for those who dared to lay hands on their master, a similar range of punishments existed depending on the seriousness of the act and the importance of the person touched.

12. David-Néel (Alexandra), *Grand Tibet et vaste Chine,* Paris, Omnibus, 1994, reed. 1999, p. 985.

The taste for black humor will be recognized by those for whom the almost identical laws defined slavery in our country and a banal "sharecropping" in Tibet.

So we count seventeen years of training in the profession, more than nine years of reign before the chafing announcement of the Dalai Lama's will, dictated by his goodness and his love of democracy, to put an end later to a feudal heritage that made the power and the opulence of fourteen Dalai Lamas and theirs.

Certainly, many French people will rightly find much to object to in the Chinese conception of democracy and the system that prevails to this day in Lhasa. But they will object even more to the discovery of what the Dalai Lama's government was and what the program of the Tibetan government in exile is.

IV
Institutionalized ignorance

"You have been trying to gag the human mind for a long time now! [...]
And you want to be the masters of teaching! [If the brain of humanity were there before your eyes at your discretion, open like the page of a book, you would make erasures [...] "[13]
"During my studies, I had only learned about our own social system and had acquired very little knowledge about those of other countries [...]"[14]

In 1963, the John Didier publishing house in Paris published the *Dalai Lama's Memoirs* with a possessive subtitle: *My Land and My People*, a work initially published in the United States in 1962 under the title *My Land and My People*[15]. The author was twenty-seven years old at the time, and he prefaced the French edition with a "Message to French readers" which he hoped would "give them a better understanding of my country.

13. Hugo (Victor), "La liberté de l'enseignement", 15 January 1850, in *Œuvres complètes. Politique*, Paris, Robert Laffont, 1985.
14. Dalai Lama, *op. cit.*
15 Dalai Lama, *My Land and My People*, New York, McGraw-Hill, 1962.

In fact, it is also the Dalai Lama that we will get to know better by reading pages where a certain political naivety vies with an early art of evasion and the acceptance of a situation whose anachronism he does not measure and which he claims was a source of felicity for all Tibetans (even for those who do not recognize his authority, but who are nevertheless automatically enrolled in his words): "Thus, at the age of four and a half, I was formally and solemnly recognized as the reincarnation of the thirteenth Dalai Lama; thus the fourteenth supreme spiritual and temporal leader of Tibet. In the eyes of the entire people, this event seemed to be a guarantee of happiness and lasting peace.[16]

From the outset, we see that the Dalai Lama reigns without sharing, having religious and political power over the entire region where three out of four branches of Buddhism do not recognize him.

This is followed by a justification of a theocracy frozen in time, refusing external progress, closed to the contribution of humans from elsewhere. In need of a euphemism, the Dalai Lama will find and systematically use the word *isolation*. What was it about? To add to the remoteness of a Tibet that is difficult to access, a cultural, scientific, ideological and xenophobic stifling that will result in the rejection of the knowledge that radiates from the other peoples of the earth, except, perhaps, a few primitive tribes buried in deep forests and whose existence is belatedly discovered. The very few Tibetans who will be able to attend a school will be force-fed Buddhism while modern sciences will not be taught. The backwardness accumulated by this insane blacklisting of the knowledge that was pulling the rest of the world out of its miserable ancestral condition is such that even today, half a century after school was made compulsory, Tibetan students are given a bonus for their grades (positive discrimination) so that their success rate in exams is comparable to that of other Chinese students.

---

16. Dalai Lama, *Memoirs of the Dalai Lama. My Land and My People, op. cit.,* p. 33.

What did the teaching "according to the traditional Tibetan system" consist of? The Dalai Lama recognizes many virtues in this system, even though it "obviously has the defect of ignoring the scientific discoveries of the past centuries, which can be explained by the fact that Tibet has only recently ceased to be entirely isolated from the rest of the world"[17]. Despite the tortuous form of the sentence (or a translation error), one understands that Tibet was closed and science was banned, and that these anomalies ended with the establishment of an administration desired by Beijing to replace the vacant power.

What were the teachings given to the Tibetans, or more precisely to the five percent of them who received them? First of all, "five minor subjects" which concern "dramatic art, dance and music, astrology, poetry, literary composition". All these subjects? No, the monk students could only study "astrology and literary composition"[18].

Then "five major subjects" which correspond to a higher education and which are: "the art of healing, the study of Sanskrit, dialectics, arts and crafts, metaphysics and religious philosophy [...] of which the last one - metaphysics and religious philosophy - is by far the most important [...]"[19] and which are themselves subdivided into five parts: perfection of wisdom, the path of the middle, the rules of the monastic discipline, metaphysics, logic and dialectics

The well-trained Tibetan scholar knows little more than the illiterate serf about what, throughout the world and over the centuries, has enriched intelligence and thought, and improved daily life. Physics, chemistry, mechanics, architecture, economics, philosophical or artistic trends and other ungodly trinkets are blocked at the gates of mystical Tibet by a deliberate policy of "isolation. No one knew or was supposed to know, or in any case was supposed to

17. *Ibid.*, p. 35.
18. *Ibid.*
19. *Ibid.*, p. 36.

teach, for example, geometry or algebra, heresies considered useful everywhere else for centuries before our era.

Of course, world history and geography were not honored either, as they were useless for the perpetuation of the theocracy, and even dangerous. Looking at an atlas of distant countries, the future leader of Tibet observed that he had "never yet met anyone who had been there"[20]. "My education in world affairs had been imperfect, and it was in this near ignorance that, at the age of sixteen, I was called to lead my country against the invaders of Communist China.[21]

Ignorance wanted, organized, guaranteeing an immobility which suits so well the ruling caste, ignorance without which the Tibetan people, "proud, courageous and warlike", according to the description that the dalaï-lama himself makes, would probably have shaken the yoke of a religious oppression unique in the world at the time when this last one reached the power. Orphaned by this revolt, which would have allowed them to keep the monks, but without their temporal power and without the parasitic aristocracy, the Tibetan people saw themselves, more than others, caught in the trap of a multiple confinement, deprived as they were of knowledge, modernity, democratic rights, non-religious justice, authorization to travel and to receive foreigners.

"In the recent past, what has most characterized us has been our isolation, which has been deliberate. [We have increased our isolation by allowing only the smallest possible number of foreigners into Tibet.[22]

"Most of the Tibetans who lived in the distant border provinces had never been to Lhasa, or even met anyone who had been there in their lives. Year after year they worked their land, raised their cattle, yaks or other animals, and no one knew what was happening beyond their own horizon."[23]

---

20. *Ibid.,* p. 50.
21. *Ibid.,* p. 51.
22. *Ibid.,* p. 54.
23. *Ibid.,* p. 59.

And how would the unfortunate people have traveled, without a penny, subjected as they were to endless days of work, obliged to endless drudgery for the nobles and the monks (one counted up to two hundred drudgeries due)? And how could they have taken the risk of moving away from their land, of giving the impression of fleeing which would be punished with unimaginable cruelty? Wang Gui, a Tibetologist who worked and lived in Tibet from 1950 to 1981, testifies for China Radio International: "Three knives struck the serfs: drudgery, taxes and interest on loans, which were too high. The peasants then had three options: exodus, slavery or begging."[24]

While visiting Tibet in the 1960s, two Americans interviewed a former serf, Tsereh Wang Tuei, who had once stolen two sheep from a monastery. For this he had his eyes enucleated and his hand mutilated. He explains that he is no longer a Buddhist[25].

The confinement and terror allowed for the maintenance of a political system of appalling injustice that could have been undermined by the revelation of other systems that existed elsewhere and that had abolished the ferocious practices that existed in Tibet. "In my studies I had only learned about our own social system and had acquired very little knowledge about those of other countries. I believe that Tibetans generally regarded ours as a natural state of affairs..."[26] the Dalai Lama naively acknowledges.

Also seen as natural, no doubt, is the plethora of clerics: "Although no statistics have ever been compiled, it is likely that at the time I ruled, ten percent of Tibetans were monks and nuns."[27] The percentage may be slightly underestimated. The Chinese authorities speak of one hundred and twenty-five thousand monks out of a population of one million at the time, which would be more than twelve percent

24. "Tibet. Emancipation of serfs a 'great victory for human rights,' experts say", CRI Online, March 18, 2009.
25. Gelder (Stuart and Roma), *The Timely Rain: Travels in New Tibet*, New York, Monthly Review Press, 1964.
26. Dalai Lama, *op. cit.*, p. 60.
27. *Ibid.*, p. 55.

of the total population. It can be said that about twenty-five percent of the male population was kept away from work and procreation.

Framed by a swarm of monks whom they exhausted themselves to feed and clothe, unaware that another world functioned differently, repressed savagely if they disobeyed, but consoled, before dying (on average around the age of thirty-five) because they would be, thanks to their sufferings, reincarnated in a life of dream, the Tibetans never started a revolution which would have been however even more necessary than the one that the French people started in 1789.

From this point of view, and whatever the view that everyone has the right to have on Mao's China, on the "cultural revolution" which attacked all the vestiges of the past (and the monasteries were in this respect all designated for the Tibetan or Han "Red Guards"), whatever the prejudices may be on today's China and on its policy towards its regions, We must recognize that the dawn of Lhasa came from Beijing, which transformed what the masters of Tibet called "talking animals" into citizens with the same rights as those of other Chinese, rights that would certainly benefit from being extended, but of which, until then, ninety-five percent[28] of Tibetans were deprived.

In the monasteries, injustice reigned in the same way. The poor young monks, taken by force from their parents at a very early age, served as servants to others. As for the nobles, they knew how to spot pretty young girls among the peasants to make them servants... of proximity.

"Those who belong to other religions often say that the belief in reincarnation - the law of karma - tends to make men accept inequalities of fortune, perhaps too meekly. This is only partly true. The poor Tibetan peasant was probably less inclined than another to envy or resent the fate of the rich landowner on whom he depended, because he knew that each person ripens the seed he had sown in

---

28. "Demography Tibet. Retrospective on the economic and social development of the last fifty years", *GeoPopulation*, Xinhua, 30 March 2009, in http://www.geopopulation.com/20090331/demographie-tibet-retrospective-sur-le-developpement-economique-et-social-des-50-dernieres-annees/

a previous life. [This is how the Tibetans accepted our social system without murmuring.[29]

They not only accepted without a murmur, they were, if one may be ironic, ecstatic: "Anyway, in spite of the defects of our social system, in spite of the harsh climate of our land, one can say that Tibet was the happiest country there is. "So we lived happily." "The dual position of the Dalai Lama as spiritual and temporal ruler...had made possible the happy administration of Tibet for three hundred years.[30] And this was all the more so because "however feudal [the system] was, it still differed from any other feudal system, because at its apex was the incarnation of Chenresi - the being whom the people had worshipped for centuries"[31].

Happy people in a Shangri-La (earthly paradise)? Wouldn't this be a case of applying the Coué method or advertising recipes? In January 2005, during his twenty-minute inaugural speech, George W. Bush used the word *freedom* forty times, an average of once every thirty seconds. In *A Human Approach to World Peace*[32], the Dalai Lama will use the word *happiness* twelve times.

But concretely, under the leadership of the Dalai Lamas, there is no bliss for Tibetans who are punished in this life because they did not succeed in a previous life, but who are promised a magnificent future life if they accept this one with abnegation!

Its two jaws firmly in place around the stainless axis of faith, it remains to bite *in secula seculorum* into the flesh of a confined and deluded people, stupefied by fatigue, blinded by ignorance, stunned by the magnificence of the monasteries, crushed by the gigantism of severe Buddha statues and drunk with prayers, a people convinced that their ordeal is part of Tibetan culture, of its traditions, and that any reform to free them from it would be akin to a sacrilege whose

29. Dalai Lama, *op. cit.* pp. 64-65.
30. *Ibid.* pp. 64, 65 and 139 respectively.
31. *Ibid.*, p. 65.
32. Dalai Lama, *A Human Approach to World Peace*, Marzens, Vajra Yogini, 1999, reprinted in *Freedom for Tibet*, Paris, L'Arganier, 2008, pp. 113-123.

salty bill would be presented to them in a future life, henceforth as hopeless as the one they endure.

Meanwhile, in Lhasa, in the Potala Palace, "one of the greatest buildings in the world", where one could "reside for a year without knowing all the secrets", which "is a city in itself [which] occupies the whole top of a hill"[33] and "has thirteen floors", one can swoon before "mausoleums of seven Dalai Lamas, almost ten meters high, covered with gold and encrusted with precious stones"[34].

The countless rooms could house a swarm of monks, guards and servants, the Buddhist school, monks' apartments, a prison "somewhat like the Tower of London"[35] and store thousands of pieces of jewelry and jade, satin garments, furs, cloaks set with pearls and precious stones and tons of food. "Entire rooms contained chests full of gold regalia that belonged to the kings of Tibet, lavish offerings that the rulers had received from the emperors of China and Mongolia, and the treasures of the Dalai Lamas who succeeded the kings.[36] "In the immense basements, endless galleries had been cut through and cellars built where stocks of butter, tea, and clothing for the army, monasteries, and government officials were stored."[37]

Already, under the thirteenth Dalai Lama, European luxury goods, fashionable clothes, imported perfumes, had been introduced without much resistance, but only in the world of the rich.

If the reign of the fourteenth Dalai Lama was too short for him to have time to pick up a pen and sign a decree abolishing the deadly injustices, the drudgery, the slavery, the practices that had lived in other countries of the world and from which most other religions (all of them, no doubt) had departed, it was long enough, however,

33. Dalai Lama, *Memoirs of the Dalai Lama. My Land and My People, op. cit.,* p. 45.
34. Dalai Lama, *op. cit.,* p. 46.
35. Dalai Lama, *op. cit.,* p. 47.
36. Dalai Lama, *op. cit.,* p. 46.
37. *Ibid.,* p. 47.

that in those "happy days"[38], he was able to expand his habitat. The Norbulinka Palace was the summer residence of all the Dalai Lamas, and each one "added his own residence. I built one myself"[39].

In the surroundings, the nourishing people die early from fatigue, malnutrition, cold, disease, and mistreatment while their leader

"[...] drink with the rich
And say to the poor: friend, come fast with me."40

38. *Ibid.*, p. 53.
39. *Ibid.*, p. 48.
40 HUGO (Victor), *Les Châtiments*, Paris, Gallimard, 1964.

V
The art of disguise

The People's Republic of China (PRC) was founded in October 1949. Its government operates under the leadership of the Communist Party. This is not a scoop, at most an indication that risks distracting us from the sole subject I want to deal with here. But if I mention it, it is so that everyone will note that, for ten years, the central communist power and the Dalai Lama coexisted.

The fourteenth Dalai Lama even held important positions within the communist apparatus. In 1954, he was elected vice-chairman of the Standing Committee of the National People's Congress. Mao Zedong himself assured him that no major reforms would be undertaken for six years in a Tibet whose identity would be preserved.

In the context of the Dalai Lama's trip to Toulouse in August 2011, the published briefing paper will downplay his assumption of responsibility in the Chinese Communist apparatus, stating only, "In 1954, he went to Beijing to try to negotiate a peace agreement with Mao Tse-Tung and other Chinese leaders, among them Chou En-lai and Deng Xiaoping."

However, in 1955, on the occasion of the New Year's celebrations in Beijing, the Dalai Lama pronounced a speech of thanks to the Chinese government before writing a poem to the glory of Mao. In 1956, he became president of the preparatory committee of the autonomous region of Tibet (RAT). The same year, in November, he went to India to participate in the ceremonies of the two thousand five hundredth anniversary of the death of the Buddha. His two elder brothers tried to convince him not to return to Tibet and to campaign for independence. It will be necessary that Chou En-lai in person comes to give him a missive of Mao promising that there would still be no changes in Tibet in the six years to come, so that the dalaï-lama postpones the opening of the hostilities.

However, the monks and the aristocrats of Lhasa, anxious for their privileges, already started to organize centers of rebellion, which burst in 1956, in Litang in Kham, spreads to the other sectors of this province, then in 1957 and 1958 to the sectors of Amdo, in 1958 and 1959 to Ü-Tsang, to the future autonomous region of Tibet, to reach Lhasa in March 1959.

As we will see, playing a double game, the Dalai Lama will secretly be the instigator of the troubles.

China is made up of twenty-two provinces, five autonomous regions, thirty autonomous prefectures and one hundred and twenty-four autonomous districts, plus one thousand three hundred ethnic townships in multi-ethnic regions.

There are thus a multitude of possibilities for the break-up of a country where about two hundred languages are spoken, including twenty-four Chinese languages.

Having to govern and feed this immense and overpopulated country, where fifty-six disparate ethnic groups live side by side, Mao Zedong, busy revolutionizing all its structures, thought it wise to postpone the reforms on Tibetan territory. Slavery, the overexploitation of the people by monks and nobles, the undivided power of the Dalai Lama, lasted for more than nine years in Communist China, which exalted the virtues of equality, education, technical and social progress against the background of Marxist theory, which was nevertheless very reluctant to subscribe to the omnipotence of religions. In the hope of avoiding bloody confrontations, the Chinese Communist Party made a soft paw and cohabited with the last feudal theocracy in the world, capable of refusing progress in any matter whatsoever.

In these times, the "isolation" of the Buddhist elites was no longer sufficient for them to ignore what was happening in the rest of China and in other countries, which could happen to them one day, because such is the logic of the world's march.

If the deprived Tibetans, who whispered that they owned only their shadow and would take only their dust with them in death, stood to gain from the implementation of a more sharing policy, their masters, nobles, monks, Dalai Lama, saw the time coming to lose their privileges and, in the worst case, to be held accountable.

From this point on, it is understandable that the rebellion against Beijing was prepared and broke out well before the clashes that forced the Dalai Lama to flee to India.

With an accomplished art of doublespeak that does not fit well with the innocence that the West knows him to be, the Dalai Lama will be the deus ex machina of the revolt, sitting in high places of the state apparatus in Beijing, glorifying Mao, assuring him that he disavows these "reactionary malefactors," these "groups of reactionaries" whose violence plunges him "into immense anxiety. He assured him that he was doing "the impossible" to resolve the situation, and that he had "educated" and "severely criticized" the insurgents. This information comes from a book published in March 2009 by the Information Office of the State Council of the People's Republic of China, and my reader will want to cross-check it with other sources. Let us see what the Dalai Lama says in his *Memoirs* about his exchanges with a Chinese general who is his interlocutor in Lhasa: "I therefore decided to write to him, giving him the impression that I readily accepted his expression of sympathy and welcomed his advice. [...] I informed him that I had given orders for the crowd to disperse"[41], all in letters that were intended to "conceal

41. Dalai Lama, *op. cit.*, p. 188.

my true intentions"[42], for it was a matter of "pretending"[43] to enter into the general's views. Thus, when the probability of a violent confrontation in Lhasa itself was becoming strong, the Dalai Lama announced by letter to the general his intention to meet him, but, he confided to his reader, "this was obviously not my intention"[44].

As an aside, we can appreciate his praise of religions which "all teach us not to lie, not to bear false witness, not to steal, not to kill, etc."[45] A belief that he will confirm almost word for word in a more recent text: "All of them teach us not to lie, not to steal, not to take the lives of others and so on."[46]

---

42. *Ibid.,* p. 189.
43. *Ibid.,* p. 192.
44. *Ibid.,* p. 193.
45. *Ibid.,* p. 246.
46. DALAI LAMA, "World Religions for Universal Peace", in *Freedom for Tibet, op. cit.,* p. 129.

VI
The art of the war called peace

Is Tibetan pacifism, atavistic, or inculcated in the people by an omnipotent religion, a reality or a myth? Let us leave it to the Dalai Lama himself to enlighten us:

"I will not pretend that Tibetans are all kind people; we also have our sinners and criminals. Among our nomadic tribes, most of whom were peaceful people, there were clans who were not incapable of committing acts of brigandage, so that some suburbanites were armed in their homes far from the centers, and travelers passing through dangerous areas preferred to travel in large groups. [For the Khampa tribe] a gun counts more than any other object."[47] Sometimes it was his entire people whose "warlike inclinations" or "instinct to fight" he feared he could not "control"[48].

Moreover, the Dalai Lama, adored by these happy people, "never travelled without an escort of twenty-five armed guards and the troop was always posted on the route"[49]. It is true that Dalai Lamas had once been assassinated by thugs commanded by relatives.

47. Dalai Lama, *Memoirs of the Dalai Lama. My Land and My People, op. cit.*, p. 60.
48. *Ibid.* pp. 151 and 240 respectively.
49. *Ibid.*, p. 176.

On his army: "In fact, it was mainly used to hold the border posts and to prevent foreigners without visas [that is, almost all foreigners, *NDA*] from entering the country. They were also our police, except in Lhasa and the monasteries, which had their own law enforcement agencies." (p. 57). "...] it totaled eight thousand five hundred officers and men. We had more than enough rifles, but our artillery consisted of only about fifty pieces of various calibers, two hundred and fifty mortars and about two hundred machine guns, representing far too little firepower to wage war."[50]

Let us observe that it is not a Gandhian love of non-violence that is invoked here, but the risk of defeat.

This analysis was taken up by the Dalai Lama almost half a century later, on May 12, 2008, when he gave an interview to the German magazine *Der Spiegel* in which the pacifism of the religious leader does not appear to be consubstantial with his thinking, but imposed by the balance of power: "Should the Tibetans take up arms to conquer this independence? What weapons, from where? From the mujahideen in Pakistan, perhaps? And if we get them, how will we get them into Tibet? And if the war of independence starts, who will help us? The Americans? The Germans?"

To this question, an answer with the scent of an appeal to the Pentagon was given by His Holiness on April 29, 2005 to French senators who came to see him in his Indian exile: "American policy wants to promote democracy in Iraq and Afghanistan, by sometimes controversial methods. I say so much the better, it is welcome. But it would be even better if democracy were promoted in China."[51]

Is the Dalai Lama a defeated general who withdraws "to positions prepared in advance"? Does he practice the art of peace, or the art of war, which is made of offensives and retreats, truces and armistices,

50. *Ibid.,* p. 82.

51. Report of the Franco-Tibetan friendship group of the Senate, June 14, 2006.

victories and defeats, propaganda and lies? It is up to the reader to decide by reading the additional information below.

At the time of his reign, his military inferiority will push him, fearing to see Peking deeply reform Tibet, to call upon foreign powers, because "Tibet had neither the material resources, nor the weapons, nor the men allowing him to defend himself against a large-scale attack". "Four delegations were formed to go to the United States, Great Britain, India and Nepal to ask these countries for their support.[52] The latter refused to respond favorably to the call for war and kept their soldiers at home. Washington "refused even to receive the members of the delegation"[53]. As a result of these "negative responses to [their] requests for military aid, the Chinese hordes could invest [them]; [they were] abandoned by all"[54].

The Dalai Lama recounts that he visited the tomb of Gandhi in India "who had a deep faith in peace and understanding among men" and asks himself: "My meditation led me to ask myself what wise advice the Mahatma would have given me [...]"[55] Perhaps that of not calling on the armies of four foreign countries to invade a Chinese province and sow death there so that it would remain mired in a theocratic gangue where power, no, *all* power would be concentrated in the hands of one man, an unquestionable spiritual and temporal leader, because it would have come about through the divine miracle of a suitable reincarnation.

The peaceful Dalai Lama having been rejected in his request for armed intervention by four foreign nations to preserve his power, what happened next? According to him, just a "peaceful uprising of Tibetans in Lhasa on March 10, 1959"...[56]

---

52. Dalai Lama, *Memoirs of the Dalai Lama. My Land and My People, op. cit.*, p. 82.
53. *Ibid.*, p. 83.
54. *Ibid.*, p. 88.
55. *Ibid.*, p. 150.
56. Statement by His Holiness the Dalai Lama on the forty-ninth anniversary of the Tibetan National Uprising Day, Dharamsala, March 10, 2008.

We have read "Pacific" correctly. On the contrary, Beijing claims that it was an armed insurrection. Who is to be believed? Let the Dalai Lama tell us about the events in his *Memoirs*.

"...] the Chinese publicly announced that a revolt had broken out in eastern Tibet and that they would do everything to break it. This news deeply moved the ministers [of the Dalai Lama] who were not unaware that the Khampas were resisting with arms [...]".[57]

"...] the number of Khampas who led the guerrilla war in the mountains had increased from a few hundred to several tens of thousands. They had fought large-scale battles [...]"[58]

"My countrymen are not people who can be bent by presence and terror, and to attempt to destroy their religion, their most precious possession, is a foolish undertaking. So there followed a worsening and extension of the revolt. While relative peace still prevailed in western and central Tibet, the people of the eastern, northeastern and southwestern provinces took up arms."[59]

"I myself was quite unhappy with the way things were going, but on the other hand I had great admiration for the insurgents, brave men and women who did not hesitate to risk the lives of their children to defend the cause of our rebellion and our country."[60]

One gets the impression from reading it that the entire population has taken up the cause of the Dalai Lama and his people in these struggles. Alexandra David-Néel is more nuanced. She affirms that the population did not resist en masse to the arrival of the Chinese army. According to her, the peasants were not completely unaware of the results obtained in China by the agrarian reforms. "They were waiting with sympathy for that which may come as a result of the Chinese troops."[61]

---

57. *Ibid.*, p. 163.
58. *Ibid.*, p. 164.
59. *Ibid.*, p. 165.
60. *Ibid.* pp. 166-167.
61. David-Néel (Alexandra), *op. cit.*, p. 1016.

When the revolt, which was thus armed and fomented behind the scenes by the Dalai Lama against the central government in Peking, failed, when his troops had to retreat to India, he would put on a uniform in a manly manner. On March 17, 1959, "at about eight o'clock in the evening, I took off my lama robe and put on a military uniform [...]". "A soldier...handed me a rifle, which I threw over my shoulder..."[62] In the hagiographic presentation of the book *Inspirations and Words of the Dalai Lama*[63], the South African journalist and writer Mike Nicol dares to say: "Ironically, it was disguised as a soldier, with a rifle on his shoulder, that he left Lhasa at night with his retinue and headed for the Indian border."[64] Let us pass over the oddity that, supposedly a pacifist during the fighting, the leader of the insurgents decided, for his "escape to Varennes", to put on a uniform and to equip himself with a rifle in order to leave more discreetly later. Usually, defeated soldiers run away disguised as civilians and "peaceful" uprisings do not need soldiers, otherwise, everywhere in the world, they are said to be "armed".

On this episode, Alexandra David-Néel reports details that the fugitive and Mike Nicol omit and which are nevertheless of the greatest importance, because it is a question of what happened to the public treasury in this miserable region: "With him went a number of civil servants; servants of various ranks and a caravan of more than a thousand mules, plus a great many porters evacuating boxes full of gold and precious objects from the Potala.[65]

62. Dalai Lama, *Memoirs of the Dalai Lama. My Land and My People, op. cit.* pp. 198 and 199 respectively.
63. *Compassion: inspirations and words of the Dalai Lama,* preface by Desmond Tutu, introduction by Mike Nicol, Paris, Acropole, coll. "Ubuntu", 2008.
64. *Ibid.,* p. 18.
65. David-Néel (Alexandra), *op. cit.* pp. 979-980.

VII
Independence or autonomy?

According to the circumstances, the places, the interlocutors and what he believes to be his interest of the moment, the Dalai Lama will ask, sometimes for an autonomy in the beloved China or a total independence, out of the hated China. Ambiguity, contradictions and reversals are legion. Is it only a question of an understandable evolution of his thinking over the years or of a permanent double talk? And finally, what does the Dalai Lama want? Independence? Autonomy? The answers are given here by excerpts from his speeches and his own writings since, let us accept this fact, those of his detractors are suspect.

The difference between a Corsican who is attached to a special status for the island and a Corsican who militates for independence is that the former will refer to the Hexagon as "the Continent". The second will say "France", emphasizing that it is a foreign country. The method applies everywhere and to everyone.

It is particularly relevant in this case, where the Dalai Lama virtually divides his country in two: on the one hand, the Tibetans, and on the other, the fifty-five other ethnic groups that make up China, whom he refers to as *Chinese* and, on occasion, as *Chinese hordes*.

Chapter 4 of his memoirs is entitled *Our Neighbor China*, which clearly indicates that China is a foreign country, as Tibet became a "fully independent nation between 1912 and 1950"[66].

"Tibet's neighbors are numerous: to the north and east, China and Mongolia; to the south, India, Burma, Nepal, Bhutan, and Sikkim. Pakistan, Afghanistan, and the USSR are also close by."[67]

One wonders here why the Dalai Lama would want Tibet to become an autonomous region of one of these "foreign" countries, in this case China.

Moreover, he does not go any further into the inextricable web of Tibet's erratic relations with China over the centuries. These relations were not linear, sometimes distended, especially when a European power (England) ruled with its army. For Alexandra David-Néel, "for centuries, the history of Tibet has been intimately linked to that of China"[68].

The Dalai Lama seems to agree: "I would not lose sight of the fact that the Chinese would claim that Tibet has always been part of China [...]" before pointing out: "despite thirty-eight years of total independence"[69].

Between the first Dalai Lama, Gedun Drub, who died in 1474, and the fourteenth Dalai Lama, Tenzin Gyatso, who reigned until 1959, almost five centuries passed during which Tibet experienced "thirty-eight years of total independence. A short independence that can only be said to be total if we forget the colonial presence of the British.

However, in the eyes of the Dalai Lama, these less than four decades of relative independence seem to weigh more heavily than five centuries of living together, which, by continuing, would undermine the racial specificity of Tibetans. This is evidenced by the Dalai

66. Dalai Lama, *Memoirs of the Dalai Lama. My Land and My People*, *op. cit.*, p. 76.
67. *Ibid.*, p. 53.
68. David-Néel (Alexandra), *op. cit.*, p. 964.
69. Dalai Lama, *Memoirs of the Dalai Lama. My Land and My People*, *op. cit.*, p. 225.

Lama's *five-point Peace Plan* addressed to the US Congressional Human Rights Committee on September 21, 1987.

The Dalai Lama pronounces himself for a rigorous racial purification by the pure and simple expulsion from "Great Tibet" of any population which would not be of Tibetan ethnicity. He estimates the number of intruders at more than six and a half million who should leave as soon as he returns. This "transfer" is for him "imperative".

The Dalai Lama's firm claim to independence and the distinction he makes between Tibetans, who are "different," and the other 55 ethnic groups in China, who are supposed to form a homogeneous whole, even though most of them have their own culture, traditions and languages, are also noteworthy. But if the Dalai Lama were to take these specificities into account, he would have to openly deduce and proclaim that China's natural destiny is to break up into a host of small states.

Let's imagine the partition of France (a nation built from scratch) by the independence of the Basque Country, Brittany, Provence, Corsica, the Nice region and the overseas departments and territories. After all, Provence became French territory in 1481, Brittany in 1532, Corsica in 1768, the county of Nice in 1860. And is it necessary to mention our distant possessions, so different from the metropolis, such as New Caledonia, a French archipelago located seventeen thousand kilometers from the Hexagon?

The idea of splintering being awkward for his personal claim, the Dalai Lama therefore opts for a dichotomous description of China.

"Open conflicts have erupted in the Middle East, Southeast Asia as well as in my own country, Tibet."

"Tibet remains an illegally occupied independent state to this day."

"Tibetans and Chinese are different peoples, each with their own country, history, culture, language and way of life."

"It is the illegal occupation of Tibet by China [...]"

"There is no doubt that when the Communist armies of Beijing invaded Tibet, it was in every respect an independent state [...]"

"In 1982, I sent my representatives to the Chinese capital [...] to open a dialogue about the future of my country and my people."

"I wish... a future of friendship and cooperation with our neighbors, including the Chinese people," etc.[70]

On December 10, 1989, in his Nobel Peace Prize acceptance speech, he informed the honorable assembly: "As you know, Tibet has been living under foreign occupation for forty years."

Old speeches, one might say, the Dalai Lama has evolved. It is true, as I have said, that his program has become more and more frayed over the years and through failures, but here and there it has been pierced by irrepressible calls for independence that spring up like a cry from the uncontrolled heart. For, in the substance of his claim, it is not the already existing autonomy of historical Tibet (the autonomous region of Tibet) that he is claiming, but rather the independence of what he calls "Greater Tibet", that is to say an immense territory grouping together regions where Tibetans have always been a minority.

In his speech "Buddhism and Democracy" (Washington D.C., April 1993), which was full of generalities about democracy, the Dalai Lama said, "For many reasons, I have decided that I will not be the leader or play a role in government when Tibet becomes independent. However, on March 10, 2008, in Dharamsala (India), he gave a speech in which he claimed that the language, customs and traditions of Tibet were gradually disappearing, and reinvested himself in the role of spokesman for the Tibetans: "[...] I have the historical and moral responsibility to continue to speak freely on their behalf." He also criticizes the organization of autonomous regions: "These places are autonomous in name only.

The French senators have seen something else in the autonomous region of Tibet:

---

70 Dalai Lama, Washington, D.C., United States Congress, September 21, 1987.

"The TAR has just over two million of the six million Tibetans living in China.

The Law on the Autonomy of Ethnic Regions of May 31, 1984, provides a general framework for all autonomous regions in China. According to this law, the People's Assembly of the Tibet Autonomous Region not only has the power to formulate local regulations, which is granted to all ordinary Chinese provinces, but also has the power to formulate autonomy regulations according to the political, economic, cultural and educational characteristics of Tibetans. The legislative body of the autonomous region can also amend and supplement certain state laws. For example, the TAR has set working hours at thirty-five hours per week, which is five hours less than the national legal working hours, taking into account Tibet's particular geographical conditions."[71]

But here is the most astonishing thing: in March 2008, in the run-up to the Beijing Olympic Games, campaigns on the Tibetan question were launched abroad (particularly in Paris, I will come back to this), which were a source of irritation to the Chinese population. The Dalai Lama would be making a major mistake if he did not distance himself from this. It is important for him to dissociate himself from those who can appear as the enemies of China and the breakers of the Olympic dream, a dream shared by the Tibetans. The Olympic flame must cross two cities of Tibet: the capital, Lhasa, and Shannan. Also, on March 28, he launches an *Appeal to the Chinese people* where we believe to dream by reading: "Chinese brothers and sisters, I assure you that I do not wish in any way to obtain the separation of Tibet nor even to scramble the Tibetan and Chinese people. And again, he expresses his concern as "a person who feels ready to consider himself a member of this great family that is the People's Republic of China," expressing surprise at the unfair suspicion: "It is unfortunate that despite my sincere efforts not to separate Tibet

71. Report of the interparliamentary friendship group of the Senate, October 17, 2007.

from China, the leaders of the People's Republic of China continue to denounce me as a 'separatist.'"

Incredible suspicion, indeed! For the Dalai Lama has never hidden from the world his love for this "great family" of which he wants to remain a member and which is composed of "invaders" (p. 98) "ruthless" (p. 164) who indulge in "plunder" (p. 94), affected as they are by a "bad education" (p. 99) which pushes them to commit "abominable" acts on Tibetans "shot, beaten to death, crucified, burned alive, hanged, strangled". 99), which leads them to commit "abominable" acts on Tibetans "shot, beaten to death, crucified, burned alive, hanged, strangled, buried alive, scalded, gutted, subjected to vivisection and decapitated" (pp. 226-227), forcing "children to shoot their fathers and mothers" (p. 227), and who "sterilized entire villages" (p. 228). On this last point, it should be noted in passing that an international commission of jurists, convened by the Dalai Lama, "studied each of the statements" (p. 228) of the Dalai Lama's and the central government's teams as well as of the "victims" in depth, without concluding that these facts were true, which does not prevent the Dalai Lama from holding them to be true (p. 228) and having them propagated. This does not prevent the Dalai Lama from believing them to be true (p. 228) and propagating them, since the Chinese are said to be "criminals" (p. 230) whose "jungle-like methods" (p. 268) have plunged Tibet "into the darkness of subjugation and oppression" (p. 275)[72].

It will be objected that here we are comparing words from 2008 with others taken from a book published in the 1960s. It is true that, in his appeal of March 2008, the Dalai Lama also showed compassion for the victims, whoever they were: Hans (he says "Chinese") or Tibetans.

---

72. Dalai Lama, *Memoirs of the Dalai Lama. My Land and My People, op. cit.*

"In light of the recent events in Tibet, I would like to share with you my thoughts on the relationship between the Tibetan and Chinese people, and make a personal appeal to each of you.

I am deeply saddened by the loss of life in the recent tragic events in Tibet and am aware that Chinese people have also died. I sympathize with the victims and their families, and I pray for them. The recent unrest clearly demonstrates the gravity of the situation in Tibet as well as the urgency of finding a peaceful and mutually beneficial solution through dialogue."

It is that times have changed. The Dalai Lama's dream of a return to China (with the help of the international community, which had to be horrified beforehand) is no longer valid, since he has realized that no armed intervention (China now has nuclear weapons) is possible. Sufficiently effective economic or commercial pressure is similarly impossible. Among the cohort of intellectuals (writers, journalists...) and politicians who have visited Tibet, some, whatever their reservations and prejudices about the Chinese system, have lifted the veil on the Tibet of yesterday and noted changes that can no longer be considered negative.

The Dalai Lama therefore adapts to the context: his language today is different from that of yesterday, without explicitly denying it. The only constant is a desire for independence, which he is tirelessly preparing for with his "government", from Dharamsala.

The publicity given in the West to this case of extermination (through sterilization and massacres) of the Tibetan population has contributed greatly to a surge of compassion for Tibet and Buddhism. However, it has been scientifically proven wrong by international experts[73].

The same goes for the figure of one million two hundred thousand deaths by violence in Tibet since the flight of the thirteenth Dalai

73. LUCON (Gérard), " Tibet, une réalité démographique et des chiffres, des chiffres... ", *Le Grand Soir*, September 17, 2010, http://www.legrandsoir.info/Tibet-une-realite-demographie-et-des-chiffres-des-chiffres.html

Lama. This figure is bogus by the "Tibetan government in exile" of the fourteenth Dalai Lama. International researchers have demonstrated this at[74]. A simple examination of the age pyramid makes it impossible to dispute this fable, which the Dalai Lama no longer supports. He no longer accuses of "genocide", but of "cultural genocide". Moreover, how can one speak of genocide of "ethnic Tibetans" (the "pure race"?) when Tibet is allowed to depart from the one-child policy in force in most Chinese regions and the population ("ethnic") has increased spectacularly since 1959?

These untruths suggest that other accounts of abuses may be false or exaggerated. Nevertheless, it would be naive and ignorant of history to swear that a military power behaves, on the ground abandoned by the fleeing rebel leaders, in a way that conforms to human rights or even to international conventions. We know how

74. A critical observer of Chinese policy, Patrick French of Britain, director of the Free Tibet Campaign, had access to the archives of the Dalai Lama's government in exile. He discovered that the evidence of the genocide was false and resigned from his position. In particular, he studied the figures collected by a brother of the Dalai Lama, Gyalo Thondrup. Among other falsifications, French found that the death toll from clashes with the Chinese army could be counted up to five times, if five refugees reported them. Thus, the death toll from Dharamsala (reported and published around the world) was to be one million two hundred thousand out of one and a half million male Tibetans at the time. The growth of the Tibetan population could only be explained by polygamy and superhuman fertility. Elisabeth Martens speaks about it in her book *Histoire du bouddhisme tibétain. La compassion des puissants*: "With a calculator in his pocket, he wanted to verify this exorbitant figure of "1.2 million victims". With bitterness, French notes in his report: "After only three days of work, it became clear that the figure of 1.2 million Tibetan deaths could not be accepted [...] The most disturbing part of this total, perhaps, was the fact that there were only 23,364 women. This would have meant that 1,076,636 victims were men, which is clearly impossible, given that there were only about 1.25 million male Tibetans in 1950 [...] It was disturbing, but I was forced to conclude that this survey [the one by the Dharamsala government], if well-intentioned, was statistically unusable and far from meeting Western requirements in this area. It was a shock!", French (Patrick), *Tibet. Une histoire personnelle d'un pays perdu*, Paris, Albin Michel, 2005.

our armies have acted in many places, in Madagascar, in Indochina, in Algeria, or even in China with the sacking of the summer palace, and our police on our own soil, in Paris itself (French Muslims thrown into the Seine in October 1961, the killings at the Charonne metro station in February 1962...). Unfortunately, it is unlikely that others are only virtues. The British subjugated Tibet by force of arms and we saw them looting, raping and destroying monasteries.

If, as the Senate report of October 2007 states, Tibet remains, as a treasure of humanity, "the eye of the world on Chinese development", it would be preferable that this eye be rid of the beam that it carries without being apparently embarrassed by it.

For his part, the Dalai Lama is wrong to ignore the crimes perpetrated over the centuries by his predecessors, crimes that are often even more cruel, proven, and accompanied by the implicit promise that the people would have to suffer them endlessly. Without end, because one does not remove a specially reincarnated authority to sit in a monastery-palace in the capital.

On April 6, 2008, spurred on by the demonstrations in Lhasa, the Dalai Lama launched an appeal "to all Tibetans" in which he swore: "I have decided to find a solution within the structure of the People's Republic of China.

Let us note that he thus demonstrates *a contrario* that the previous solutions he was looking for were located "outside the structure", which we had understood for a long time.

On November 24, 2008, the Nouvel-obs.com titled : " Dalaï-lama : Tibetans in exile are in "great danger" ". Why?

"In the next twenty years, if we are not careful, if we are not prudent in our plans, there is a great danger," the Dalai Lama warned on Sunday, November 23, in a statement to more than five hundred delegates from around the world, gathered for a week in Dharamsala. "This could lead to the danger of failure." In short, we are not much more certain. "Tibetan delegates closed their week-long meeting on Saturday by announcing that they had set aside the demand for independence for the time being, choosing to follow the "middle path" advocated by the Dalai Lama, who supports the idea of autonomy as a reasonable compromise."[75]

One thinks of the fox in the fable that cannot reach the grapes: "They are too green, he says"...

So let us see what he calls the "middle way", a proposal that he presents as innovative, conciliatory, acceptable to the power that governs China. In his speech to the European Parliament in Strasbourg on 24 October 2001, he explained that this proposal was to replace the "17-point agreement" signed with the central government in 1951 (under duress, he said), in which he saw "so-called autonomy". This agreement obliged the Beijing government on essential matters, since it committed itself "not to modify the existing political system in Tibet, not to change the status of the powers of the Dalai Lama, to respect the religious beliefs, customs and traditions of the people, to protect the monasteries, to develop agriculture, to improve the standard of living of the Tibetans and not to impose reforms on them by force"[76]. This is already not so bad! It is however the refusal of this agreement which pushed the nobles and the Buddhists to foment the revolt which ended in exile.

In his proposal of October 24, 2001, also known as the "Strasbourg proposal," the Dalai Lama asks that Tibet be allowed "genuine autonomy within the structure of China itself. This is not the paper autonomy envisaged in the "17-point agreement" that was imposed on us 50 years ago. It is about genuine autonomy for Tibet, with Tibetans fully responsible for their own domestic affairs, religious matters, culture, care of their fragile and precious environment, and the local economy. Beijing would retain responsibility for foreign policy and defense.

---

75 "Dalai Lama : Tibetans in exile are in "great danger", NouvelObs.com, November 24, 2008, http://tempsreel.nouvelobs.com/actualite/monde/20081123.OBS2245/dalai-lama-les-tibetains-en-exil-sont-en-grand-danger.html

76. Dalai Lama, *Memoirs of the Dalai Lama. My Land and My People, op. cit.* pp. 90-91.

If this is autonomy, reasoners will ask, how can independence be defined! It is as if the Dalai Lama parodied Beaumarchais' *Figaro* as follows: "Provided that you do not concern yourselves with the economy, laws, social affairs, culture, education, religion, justice, the environment, or anything else that might conflict with my decisions taken by virtue of my divine power, you can co-manage Tibet with me, especially if you stay outside to protect my borders and commercial interests under the watchful and critical gaze of the community of nations. "

A demonic mind, pretending to consider that this sharing is equitable, neither party being better served than the other since it is a "middle way", halfway between independence and annexation, could play at reversing the prerogatives that are supposed to weigh the same: to Lhasa what it concedes to Beijing, to Beijing everything else, that is, everything that allows the coalman to claim to be the sole master of his house, the aspiring coalman in saffron robes specifying in this case that his house covers the whole region, or even some surrounding areas.

Who knows why Beijing sees this proposal as a ruse, a repudiation, and why it refuses even to receive a delegation to discuss it? Perhaps because the delegation would represent a government headed by the Dalai Lama, who at the same time swears that he does not want the "separation of Tibet" because he considers himself "a member of the great family that is the People's Republic of China. Such contradictions have prompted the Chinese government to demand greater clarity by inviting the Dalai Lama to agree to an unavoidable condition for being received: the dissolution of his "government", whose existence would make his visit to China that of a *de facto* recognized foreign head of state.

Go and find out why, when the Dalai Lama claims for himself and his people the full responsibility of culture, the voice of Victor Hugo, still him, still resounds in our ears, rumbling against all the obscurantisms which freeze the thought and the progress:

"Ah, we know you! We know the clerical party. It is an old party with a record of service. (Laughter.) It is this party that stands guard at the door of orthodoxy. (Laughter.) It is this party that has found for truth those two wonderful props, ignorance and error. It is he who forbids science and genius to go beyond the missal and who wants to cloister thought in the dogma. All the steps that the intelligence of Europe has taken, it has taken in spite of him. Its history is written in the history of human progress, but it is written on the back. (Sensation.) He opposed everything. (Laughter.)

It was he who had Prinelli beaten for having said that the stars would not fall. It was he who put Campanella to the test seven times for asserting that the number of worlds was infinite and for having glimpsed the secret of creation. It was he who persecuted Harvey for proving that blood circulates. By Joshua, he locked up Galileo; by Saint Paul, he imprisoned Christopher Columbus. (Sensation.) To discover the law of heaven was impiety; to find a world was heresy. (Very good! Very good!) It was he who anathematized Pascal in the name of religion, Montaigne in the name of morality, Molière in the name of morality and religion. (Very good! Very good!) Oh yes, certainly, whoever you are, whoever you call the Catholic party and whoever you are the clerical party, we know you. For a long time now, the human conscience has been revolting against you and asking you: what do you want from me? For a long time now you have been trying to gag the human spirit! (Cheers on the left.)

And you want to be the masters of education!"[77]

It was already a century and a half ago, but we believe to see a Hugolian finger flying over Lhasa and Dharamsala to sweep a skewer of fourteen Dalai Lamas.

Do we need more examples, not from the central government in Beijing, but from the mouth or the pen of the Dalai Lama, to understand that the struggle for independence and for a theocratic Tibet of which he would be the leader has not stopped for a second, but that only the way of carrying it out fluctuates according to circumstances?

---

77. Hugo (Victor), "La Liberté de l'enseignement", *op. cit.*

VIII
The appalling regime of the Dalai Lamas

"The domination exercised by the monks of Tibet is absolute. It is a typical example of a clerical dictatorship."[78]

Promotion was easier for the monks and the religious administration: "Some were granted plots of land, others received gifts. Some became lenders at usurious rates that I did not always approve of."[79] We will regret here that the figures are not given. They varied between twenty and fifty percent. If this was not enough, the monks received subsidies from the government in the form of foodstuffs "or certain sums were taken from the taxes paid by the laity"[80].

"The inequality that presided over the distribution of wealth was certainly incompatible with the principle of Buddhist teaching, and

78. Harrer (Heinrich), Nazi officer, tutor of the Dalai Lama, *Sept ans d'aventures au Tibet*, Paris, Arthaud, 2008.
79. Dalai Lama, *Memoirs of the Dalai Lama. My Land and My People, op. cit.* p. 56.
80. *Ibid.*, p. 57.

during the brief years that I actually spent in power, I took steps to obtain certain fundamental reforms."[81]

Namely, that the "brief years" were nine in number, that he was quite young (too young) but had a regent and advisors, and that he seemed mature enough to make decisions himself (such as expanding his huge habitat), which he boasts of in order to emphasize his early wisdom. As for "some" "fundamental" reforms, it would have been useful if they had been cited and if the Dalai Lama had specified whether or not the "measures to achieve them" had been successful.

Nevertheless, we learn that he created a fifty-member commission and that the "simplest" reform was that of taxes. Indeed, in addition to governmental taxes, the district authorities "could levy as many additional taxes as they wished. [This practice was permitted by law, and the people submitted to it and paid"[82]. What kind of taxes? Here we touch on the ubiquitous: on marriages, on births, on deaths, on planting a tree in front of their house, on their animals, on religious holidays, on singing, dancing, drumming, ringing bells, on crossing a village, on entering prison, on leaving prison, on unemployment, etc. "The people submitted and paid" all the more willingly because they knew what it cost them to disobey. The proceeds of this legal robbery were replaced by a salary paid to the collectors by Lhasa (again with money taken from the people).

As the land on which the serfs were working was state property, a rent was owed to the state, which was often paid by a portion of the meager crops. "This was one of the main sources that fed the government stocks, which were distributed to the army, monasteries and civil servants." The others paid in hours of work (corvées) or "provided free transport for government officials and sometimes for representatives of the monasteries"[83]. It was a matter of serfs and slaves carrying burdens on their backs, which exempted the

81. *Ibid.,* p. 60.
82. *Ibid.,* p. 71.
83. *Ibid.,* p. 61.

fragile monks, soldiers and officials. On their backs, always and everywhere, because the use of the wheel (an invention dating from 3500 BC) was forbidden. There was no question of allowing even wheelbarrows (used in the rest of China since a century before our era) or carts pulled by animals, because they would "leave scars on the sacred surface of the earth". Not only did men wear themselves out and die, but trade was curtailed, living standards stagnated, and there were no roads in Tibet, except for a ribbon on the Red Hill of the Potala in Lhasa for the thirteenth Dalai Lama to play with in his three automobiles, which probably had the divine power not to damage anything at all. Nevertheless, bicycles and mopeds will appear during his lifetime. In 1943, the regent of the fourteenth Dalai Lama (the latter was eight years old) once again forbade the use of bicycles and mopeds, under the pretext already mentioned, which the monks were responsible for spreading. Moreover, there was no question of tracing communication routes. When the British occupants wanted to risk it, it was explained to them that the sky would be offended and would punish the neighborhood[84].

However, "the right to benefit from these transports [having] been extended to too many people", the drudgery only increasing from one dalai-lama to another, the fourteenth, in an impulse that was at once democratic, compassionate as well as measured, decided not to abolish this abomination, but to increase the fares for transports that were not compulsory drudgery and to subject them to a "special authorization"[85].

"The most urgent reform" concerned the powers of the landowners who, it should be noted in passing, had, like monks in monasteries, a "feudal right of justice. Alas, while the Dalai Lama, having received the reports of the reform commission, was considering, he said, dispossessing these large landowners of the land which had been

84. Candler (Edmund), *The Unveiling of Lhasa*, New Delhi, Pentagon Press, 1987, reprinted 2007.
85.. Dalai Lama, *Memoirs of the Dalai Lama. My Land and My People, op. cit.* p. 62.

granted to them in the past as a loan[86] and which "would be distributed to the peasants who cultivated it", he was even considering, but in a second stage the "Chinese" had crushed the revolt he was leading underhand, had seized the power left vacant by his flight, and these "invaders" deprived him of the pleasure of putting an end to the "defects of our social system", which he reports nicely as follows: "The political situation paralyzed our efforts."[87]

Interrupted in his task, the Dalai Lama does not underestimate the work he was able to accomplish: "We had, nevertheless, begun to make changes to modernize our medieval social system.[88]

But what was this medieval social system? The Dalai Lama dodges the answer. And we understand him. Thirteen Dalai Lamas before him, and he himself for nine years, made do with (took advantage of) a stultifying, brutal, genocidal system, which, even if it had been minimally reformed by his predecessor, even if he had himself trimmed some of its sharp edges, remained an insult to democracy. We are waiting today to know in what way he condemns it or in what way he finds it gentler than the one that was put in place after his flight, the one he never ceases to denounce to the whole world as a hell succeeding a paradise ("we lived happily").

Genocidal system of yesteryear? The backward theocracy was so ruthless that the population had stagnated under it at little more than a million for two centuries, which, with the early mortality of the serfs and the devout abstinence of a quarter of the men, put the Tibetan people in danger of extinction in the event of epidemic or famine. The introduction into Tibet, by the British, of qualified doctors with modern scientific knowledge, who everywhere else relieved pain, cured diseases, and delayed the fatal deadline, met with the hostility of the monks. The so-called ethnic genocide, of which it is claimed that the Tibetan people were victims because of

86. *Ibid.,* p. 63.
87. *Ibid.,* p. 64.
88. *Ibid.*

the central government in Peking, lurked, real, palpable, around the miserable villages where years passed, then decades, then centuries, without the pain of the miserable families who survived there ever being alleviated.

Dulling? Yes, because the education, considered vector of atheism and secularism, was refused to the common people while a Buddhist elite bathed in interminable studies from which could spout, to impress the serfs, a jargon which they could not understand and which persuaded them of their inferiority, feeling preliminary to humility and obedience. Dulling, because the Buddhist texts were substituted to any other kind of knowledge in the people and even in the biggest part of the lords and masters to whom the sciences had never been taught. And here, too, when the British occupiers began to open schools, the monks expressed their disagreement.

Was it still boring? Yes, because the serfs could not travel, not even to go to Lhasa, and they never saw a foreigner carrying another culture and other knowledge in their life. Finally, it was also very debilitating because the poor, exhausted men no longer had the strength and the time to think for themselves. One is tempted to define the Dalai Lama as the leader of a religion or a philosophy that has almost been degraded to the level of a sect, ruling over a million captive followers in a closed territory, sheltered from the eyes of the world.

Did I write *sect*? The word will sound strong. What is a sect? In two words, it is an organization with religious connotations, extremist and intransigent, whose leaders restrict all the individual liberties of their followers, force them to perform rituals and manipulate them mentally in order to keep them under control. The organization is pyramidal, the powers centralized in the hands of a charismatic authority: a guru. Kept in ignorance of other doctrines or practices, the faithful are subjected to conditions of existence that exhaust them (lack of rest, food, multiple tasks) and inhibit their intellectual capacities. The sect enriches itself by stripping them of their property and money, making them entirely dependent on it.

Sect or not (to each one to decide. The association Info-Sectes does not pronounce itself, while following the subject closely), brutality and plundering were the rule. This is how insolent fortunes are built:

"The Drepung monastery was one of the largest landowners in the world, with one hundred and eighty-five manors, twenty-five thousand serfs, three hundred large pastures, and sixteen thousand shepherds. The wealth of the monasteries went to the highest ranking lamas, many of whom were the offspring of aristocratic families. Secular leaders also did well. A notable example is the commander-in-chief of the Tibetan army who owned four thousand square kilometers of land and three thousand five hundred serfs. He was also a member of the Dalai Lama's inner cabinet."[89]

The serfs belonged to their lord who could punish them, sell them. They did not have the right to leave his land. They had to get his permission to marry. They could be demoted to the rank of slaves. If they proved to be unruly, they were punished: wooden cages, leg irons, shackles, tongues, hands or feet cut off, eyes gouged out (the scars were made with boiling oil), put to death by confinement in a leather bag thrown into the river. To escape this justice, they had to walk upright, pay innumerable taxes (see above), perform chores that sometimes took up to eighty percent of their working time, and provide quintals of grain to the lords. Their misery was such that they had to borrow money from the caste of monks, nobles and landowners to pay for the food they had produced and which rightfully belonged to the three orders. Usurious rates made them debtors for life, and their debts could even accumulate over entire generations through a kind of negative inheritance that was widespread. The Preparatory Committee of the Tibet Autonomous Region, a working body created by Beijing and with which the Dalai Lama was associated, cancelled these debts on July 17, 1959, a few months after the flight into exile.

---

89. GELDER (Stuart and Roma), *op. cit.*

The harshness of the climate and the aridity of the land were not overcome by new knowledge in agriculture since no one could enter Tibet to bring modern techniques or tools. The yields were disastrous. The cattle and sheep herd had too high a mortality rate to develop. Typhoid fever was killing on a large scale.

Between 1927 and 1952, the number of families braving reprisals by fleeing to seek salvation outside Tibet sometimes reached more than ninety percent in some villages. "We were living happily," said the Dalai Lama, "and I was going to undertake reforms.

It is fair to say that his predecessor, the thirteenth Dalai Lama, without going so far as to put an end to serfdom and slavery, had forbidden some of the cruellest abuses, abolishing the death penalty in 1898 (1981 in France), at least on paper, since executions did take place afterwards. In 1923, he founded the first English school in Gyantse, the country's third largest city. But it had to be closed just three years later, following a movement of obscurantist opposition from monks heated by their long training to reject progress and foreigners.

From the fourteenth Dalai Lama's *Official Translation of the Guidelines for Future Tibet's Polity and Basic Features of Its Constitution, Which His Holiness Issued on 26 February 1992*, we learn that Tibet has a recorded history of more than two thousand years, and according to archaeological discoveries, its civilization goes back more than four thousand years. How then can we explain that, in the first half of the 20th century, this region is still so ignorant of the discoveries that have spread throughout the world over the years? Because of its particular geographical situation? In part, no doubt. However, the seas and oceans are full of equally (or more) isolated territories where progress has penetrated. Added to this is a deliberate desire to petrify a society, to freeze its politico-religious system in a configuration profitable to a minority which, in its happy and prosperous Middle Ages, feared that the slightest slip of the black bandage of ignorance would reveal that, in France, in Europe and in many other countries, the Age of Enlightenment had sown new ideas on the government of human societies and that the fate of the poor had been transformed.

The scholars, philosophers, writers, involved in the production of these ideas, educated the criticism of absolutism, claimed that the private interests had to be subordinated to the general interest, that it was necessary to support the economic progress and a secular humanism, to spread everywhere the teaching, to generalize the techniques, to fight all the prejudices. These heretics professed the primacy of talents over the privileges of birth. They claimed to give meaning to the world and to find the intellectual tools to transform it. They affirmed that reason can and must reject the habits, customs and laws that undermine justice.

This plague was not to come and defile Tibet. Nevertheless, as the years went by, the Dalai Lama's regent, his advisers and the aristocrats, concerned with their own comfort, realized that they needed a few educated Tibetans who understood English to operate equipment such as a hydroelectric plant or radio transmitters. In this wonderful country, the level of technical backwardness was such that there was not a single citizen able to do this. As a result (and in desperation?), a modest school was opened in Lhasa in the middle of the summer of 1944 where instruction was given in Tibetan and English.

The regent explained that the measure was a continuation of the policy of the thirteenth Dalai Lama, but the monks were so indignant that it had to be closed six months later.

We have not read anything from the Dalai Lama in which he took exception to this with concrete measures. The illiteracy of his "happy" people had apparently not bothered him, and the few reforms he boasted of having enacted did not concern a program to set up schools in Tibet.

Will I be reproached for not comparing the ideas of the Dalai Lama of 1959 with those he may profess half a century later, in his age of wisdom? Alas, the comparison will not reassure the partisans of a secular, free and compulsory school and the development of scientific knowledge. As an international traveler, speaking to others than to an illiterate people indoctrinated by one hundred thousand monks and more, springing from two thousand seven hundred monasteries, the Dalai Lama can certainly not chant the praises of an ignorance that made the fortune of his people. So, without asserting old prejudices adorned with the shimmering shawl of the absolute supremacy of the spiritual over the material, he speaks of education without ever getting enthusiastic about its miracles and without ever omitting to denounce its perverse aspects. He applies the balanced recipe of the lark's pie: a lark of approval of the education which brings vile material comfort, a horse of regret of the blessed time when bloomed in the fields of ignorance (implicitly: thanks to it) the mental virtues favourable to happiness.

In his Nobel Peace Prize acceptance speech on December 10, 1989, even as he spoke in a place where the highest awards are given to minds that have excelled in many sciences, the Dalai Lama said, "Certainly material progress is important for human evolution. In Tibet, we have paid very little attention to the issues of economics and technology. Today we realize what a mistake that was. Having thus soberly swept away what he modestly calls an "error" (the deliberate deficiencies in education), which he believes to be limited to two sciences (in truth, all of them were affected), the Dalai Lama speaks at length about love, goodness, inner joy, calm, quietness, deep peace, serenity, all of which he identifies as being under threat: "On the other hand, material development without spiritual evolution is just as risky. There are countries that devote all their attention to external conditions and very little to internal development. Both seem important to me and must go hand in hand, ensuring a judicious balance between the one and the other [...]", etc. The paragraphs then follow one another, telling us in filigree that the knowledge likely to generate technological progress is necessarily without conscience and therefore "ruin of the soul". Does he know that history is full of examples where entire peoples, educated by books, guided by the most learned among them, have set themselves on fire for altruistic projects: for peace, justice, love of the weakest, solidarity, the right to happiness for all (and not for a caste)?

In the document quoted above (*Official Translation of the Guidelines for Future Tibet's Polity and Basic Features of Its Constitution*), the Dalai Lama laments, "Although technological advances have brought material prosperity to many people today, they have also brought about the loss of respect for human beings."

Everyone will observe that the Dalai Lama does not question an economic system that hardens the relationships between individuals and peoples. It is the technologies that are denounced. We should therefore forget that at the time when the Dalai Lamas kept their people away from any progress, innovation or instruction, Tibet was plagued by nomadic tribes forming "clans that were not incapable of committing acts of brigandage, so much so that some suburbanites were armed in their homes"[90]. He continues: "Human beings also lost much of their freedom, so that they became the slaves of machines."[91]

One could almost believe that the wheel has enslaved these Tibetans, who were once free porters in a country that was "the happiest in the world". One should almost forget that it is not a mad love, an unreasoned passion that links men to their machines, but the laws of work, of profit, laws whose imperfections the Dalai Lama never vilifies, nor do we ever hear him preach for less work and more free time, except undoubtedly for the monks exempted from any productive activity and available one hundred percent for meditation.

Let's take up his text already quoted, *A Human Approach to World Peace*. After having soberly stated (and why does he think he has to do so?) "I am not at all opposed to science and technology", the Dalai Lama will dwell, on several occasions, on their disadvantages. Through them, "we expose ourselves to lose contact with those

90. Dalai Lama, *Memoirs of the Dalai Lama. My Land and My People, op. cit.*, p. 60.
91. *Ibid.*

human aspects of knowledge and understanding that inspire us with honesty and altruism". "Science and technology, though capable of bringing immeasurable material comfort, cannot replace ancestral spiritual and humanitarian values [...]" Certainly, and there are probably millions of us, far from the advertising agencies, who can say the same thing. But, "Education may be unprecedented, but this universal education seems to have stimulated, not goodness, but mental agitation and discontent."

In *Histoire d'un bon bramin,* a tale that seems to have been written for the Dalai Lama, Voltaire describes a traveler's encounter with a Hindu priest who was watching an old woman. She "believed in the metamorphoses of Vitsnou with all her heart, and, as long as she could sometimes have water from the Ganges to wash herself, she believed herself to be the happiest of women. The priest confides: "I have said to myself a hundred times that I would be happy if I were as foolish as my neighbor, and yet I would not want such happiness." The author then poses this famous aphorism: "I would not have wanted to be happy on condition of being a fool" and he concludes: "I could not find anyone who would accept the bargain of becoming a fool in order to become happy."

Will it be permitted to prefer on this point the Voltairian wisdom of 1761 to that of the Dalai Lama, that is to say the Tibet of today to that of yesterday?

IX
A SPONSOR NAMED CENTRAL INTELLIGENCY SERVICE (CIA)[92]

You don't have to be a conspirator to see the CIA where it hides under the spidery veils of screen organizations.

In France, in the sixties, the Congress for the Freedom of Culture was an international movement of "free and independent" intellectuals who fought against Stalinism, and who published two reviews. Raymond Aron, the philosopher and "intimate enemy" of Jean-Paul Sartre, was one of its most brilliant and best known leaders. In his *memoirs*[93], he recounts his confusion when he discovered that the association was partly financed by American funds, indirectly from the CIA.

Under the name of NED (National Endowment for Democracy) hides one of the other arms of the CIA, which in the eighties financed a far-right student union, the UNI. Today, it is one of the CIA's front offices that subsidizes Reporters Without Borders, a French NGO

---

92. The information on this subject is partly taken from my book, VIVAS (Maxime), *La Face cachée de Reporters sans frontières. De la CIA aux faucons du Pentagone*, Paris, Aden, 2007.

93. ARON (Raymond), *Memoirs. 50 ans de réflexion politique*, 2 vols, Paris, Julliard, 1983.

that was at the forefront of the anti-Chinese offensive that disrupted the passage of the Olympic torch in Paris in April 2008[94]. The Dalai Lama has also been subsidized for decades by the CIA and the NED, which sponsors a host of organizations tasked with undermining China, *via* Tibet.

But what is the NED?

The American intelligence and subversion center cannot directly subsidize organizations or programs that must appear national and free or they will be discredited. It must therefore, as far as possible, use intermediaries such as the NED, which is not a private agency, but a governmental one. Its money comes from the State Department, which is a foreign policy arm of the presidency, just like the CIA. In Congress, Republicans and Democrats are in lockstep regarding the CIA's activities. The government decides, senators (of all stripes) vote, and corporate fronts collect and redistribute: "The NED was created fifteen years ago to do publicly what the CIA did surreptitiously for decades."[95]

NED's first president, Carl Gershman, admitted in 1986: "It would be terrible for democratic groups around the world to be seen as subsidized by the CIA...It was because we couldn't continue to do that that the foundation [NED] was created."[96] For his part, Allen Weinstein, who worked on the drafting of the NED's statutes in 1983, confided to the *Washington Post* on September 22, 1991, "A lot of what we do now was done in secret by the CIA twenty-five years ago."

In Nicaragua, in order to intervene in the elections that saw the defeat of the Sandinistas in February 1990, the CIA and the NED set up a so-called civic front (Via Civica). In Venezuela, the NED's budget quadrupled in the months leading up to the April 2002 coup against President Hugo Chavez. After the collapse of the Soviet Union, the

94. See the following chapters.
95. Broder (John M.), "Political meddling by outsiders: Not new for U.S.," *New York Times*, March 31, 1997.
96. *New York Times*, June 1, 1986.

NED was active in a number of Eastern countries where a government hostile to Russia and favourable to NATO could be established.

Most of the historical figures of the CIA have at one time or another sat on the board of directors or at the head of the NED, including John Negroponte, who was then appointed ambassador to occupied Iraq, and then, on his return to the United States, *big chief* of all the American intelligence services (in this capacity, he was responsible for appointing the director of the CIA)

The NED website[97] offers three dossiers on its work in China: "China (Hong Kong)", "China (Tibet)", "China (Xinjiang)".

Not to mention its covert operations (of which, by definition, we know nothing), the CIA intervenes in Tibet, *via* the NED, through no less than sixteen multiple programs that it openly subsidizes[98] : Bodkyi Translation and Research House *(fifteen thousand dollars)*, Samdup Consultations *(fifty thousand dollars)*, Gu-Chu-Sum Movement of Tibet *(forty-three thousand six hundred and seventy-five dollars)*, International Campaign for Tibet (ICT) *(fifty thousand dollars)*, International Tibet Support Network *(forty-five thousand dollars)*, Khawa Karpo Tibet Culture Centre *(twenty-five thousand dollars)*, Students for a Free Tibet *(twenty-two thousand five hundred and six dollars)*, Tibet Museum *(fifteen thousand dollars)*, Tibetan Centre for Human Rights and Democracy (TCHRD) *(fifty thousand dollars)*, Tibetan Institute for Performing Arts (TIPA) *(fifteen thousand dollars)*, Tibetan Literacy Society *(thirty-five thousand dollars)*, Tibetan Parliamentary and Policy Research Centre (TPPRC) *(fifteen thousand dollars)*, Tibetan Review Trust Society *(twenty-five thousand dollars)*, Tibetan Women's Association (Central) *(fifteen thousand dollars)*, Voice of Tibet *(thirty-three thousand six hundred dollars)*, Welfare Society Tibetan Chamber of Commerce *(fifteen thousand dollars)*.

This is the tip of the iceberg.

97. http://www.ned.org/
98. http://www.ned.org/, January 2011.

The names of these programs and organizations should not be misleading. On many occasions, U.S. propaganda has demonstrated its ability to speak in antiphrasis, to name the worst bloodthirsty dictatorships "democracies" and to advocate freedom by multiplying the number of prisons around the world, from Bagram (Afghanistan) to Abu Ghraib (Iraq) to Guantanamo (Cuba), to which must be added the impressive number of prisons in the U.S. itself, as well as secret "floating prisons. It should be noted in passing that, according to a study carried out by the International Centre for Prison Studies at King's College University in London, "with two million prisoners, or 714 prisoners per 100,000 inhabitants, the United States has the highest incarceration rate in the world, ahead of Russia and Belarus"[99].

But back to the dollars. Since his flight from China, the Dalai Lama has benefited, without bragging about it, from CIA grants.

From 1959 to 1972, one hundred and eighty thousand dollars were personally paid to him each year. He has long denied this truth. But the United States, which has many faults, has the enviable quality of having laws on declassification of accounting documents after a period of time that varies with the nature of these documents. In 1998, the documents having spoken, the Dalai Lama's "government" had to admit what was made public, merely denying that His Holiness had "personally" benefited from this money, while his representative in Washington declared that he knew neither of this grant nor of its use. On the links between the CIA and the Dalai Lama, however, he conceded: "It's an open secret, we don't dispute it."[100] Ah, how admirably these things are said: we confess because everyone knows!

The Dalai Lama also received one million seven hundred thousand dollars to carry out his international political activities. Subsequently, the same amount was paid *through* the NED.

---

99 AFP, June 27, 2005.

100. "CIA gave aid to Tibetan exiles in `60s, files show," *Los Angeles Times*, September 15, 1998.

In *Le Monde diplomatique,* Martine Bulard writes: "[...] the financing of the Tibetan organization by the CIA is not a fantasy of the Chinese communists: in the sixties, the American agency would have paid one million seven hundred thousand dollars, and the investigation of the *New York Times* ("Dalai-lama group says it got money from CIA", October 2, 1998) speaks of an annual subsidy - modest, nevertheless significant - of one hundred and eighty thousand dollars paid directly to the religious leader, who denied it.[101]

101. BULARD (Martine), "Défendre le Tibet sans (forcément) encenser le dalaï-lama", *Le Monde diplomatique,* August 2008.

X
The Olympic flame and some rabid Tibetans

> "To say it in the language of May 68, it is necessary "to foutre the brothel in Beijing". That is to say that during the Olympics we jump, we run, we swim and at the same time we need citizen athletes who say with armbands, with orange scarves, symbols of the revolution in Ukraine, their solidarity with Tibet.[102]

Reporters Without Borders, based in Paris, claims to be an NGO that defends journalists and press freedom around the world. It was created with journalists who quickly left the organization, leaving it in the hands of Robert Ménard, who, after abortive studies in philosophy, had vegetated in honey-making and then door-to-door insurance placement, before being tempted by the media.

The RSF website states: "Our action is relayed on five continents thanks to its national sections (Austria, Belgium, Canada, France, Germany, Italy, Spain, Sweden and Switzerland), its offices in New York, Tokyo and Washington, and its network of more than one

102. Daniel Cohn-Bendit, Member of the European Parliament.

hundred and twenty correspondents" relying on local associations in some fifteen countries.

RSF has luxurious premises in Paris. It employs twenty-three people, has a budget of three million seven hundred and eighty thousand eight hundred and seventy euros, of which only twenty-two thousand euros come from membership fees, i.e. less than 0.6% of its income. For the rest, it receives subsidies and various aids from large French companies, the government, the European Union, the USA, and it constantly appeals to the generosity of citizens. Among the French companies, the hypermarket Carrefour... which multiplies its stores in China. Without giving the amount, RSF indicates that the European Commission grants it credits, part of which is intended to support the action of Chinese anti-government bloggers.

What the French public doesn't know, who believe they are defending press freedom by buying agendas, calendars, photo albums, badges, comics, bags, DVDs, T-shirts, etc. from the RSF grocery store, is that the year before the Olympic flame passed through Paris, which he tried to disrupt, Robert Ménard was invited to China by the Chinese government, What the French public doesn't know is that the year before the Olympic flame passed through Paris, Robert Ménard was invited to China by the Chinese government, that he was received as a distinguished guest and that things were said and shown to him which, without being convincing enough to make this former anarchist, former Trotskyist, former socialist, former Sarkozyist, join the Chinese Communist Party, could have erased his usual Manicheism.

In a book published after the games, he claims that during his short stay in China, his hosts made a series of commitments: "Finally, we agree on a text. We stop our campaign and they release the dissidents - starting with Zao Yan, a contributor to the *New York Times*, release of prisoners, relaxation of Internet control, new working rules for foreign correspondents, and the possibility for Reporters Without Borders to visit the prisons where journalists are held, as well as to open an office in Beijing. A real deal."[103] This is a feat that all the diplomatic corps in the world and all the international associations interested in the evolution of democracy in China have not been able to achieve in several years of efforts. However, he was disappointed when he returned to Paris: "The Chinese media published our agreement while evading the part concerning the commitments of the authorities![104]

I tried in vain to obtain the text of this agreement. The Chinese embassy in Paris denies its existence and RSF has not been able to provide it to me, limiting itself to offering me a "press release" of January 23, 2007, written in Paris, which has nothing to do with a bilateral agreement and which does not include the precise points listed by Robert Ménard in his book. In this communiqué, RSF claims to wish that the Olympic Games are "a success, an opportunity for all participating countries to share the humanistic values of the Olympic spirit". It hides then that it fights since six years already to prevent the unfolding in China.

On June 13, 2001, the French site Dalai-Lamist Tibet-Info informed that "for Mr. Menard, organizing the Olympic Games in Beijing is "as monstrous" as having organized them in 1936 in Nazi Germany". At the time, RSF was not campaigning for a boycott of the opening ceremony of the Games, but simply for them not to take place in Beijing. The same site specifies that RSF sent "a file to the one hundred and twenty-three members of the IOC: *In the name of human rights, no to the candidature of Beijing 2008*, in which one can read that the choice of Beijing would be "a risky bet", because China "is a country both repressive and unstable"".

RSF, for reasons of its own, went further than the Dalai Lama who never publicly pronounced himself for a boycott of the Games or of the opening ceremony.

103. Ménard (Robert), *Des libertés et autres chinoiseries*, Paris, Robert Laffont, 2008, p. 85.
104. *Ibid.*

In Paris and elsewhere, Robert Ménard deployed a relentless activism, throwing all the forces of his organization into a project: to engage France in the disruption of the Olympic Games. He succeeded all the better because he was riding a Tibet-mania wave where the mysticism of some bobos was in conflict with their ignorance of what the Tibet of the Dalai Lamas was and what it might be tomorrow if their fight won. Filled with folklore and anti-Chinese sentiments, a few hundred troublemakers were agitated in Paris in April 2008, galvanized by certainties that they had never thought to confront with other existing contradictory approaches: testimonies of writers and journalists (there are some who report what they know), reports of parliamentarians, works of historians, sociologists, anthropologists, and even Buddhologists.

In Paris in April, the complicity of Bertrand Delanoë, the capital's mayor, was appreciated by the troublemakers. He had a chilly banner put up on City Hall: "Paris defends human rights everywhere in the world." A few days later, he will make the Dalai Lama an "honorary citizen" of the city of Paris. The green elected officials unfurled the Tibetan flag as well as a square of fabric where the rings of the Olympics are replaced by handcuffs. Robert Ménard and some mountaineers have fixed the same black sheet on Notre-Dame de Paris, etc. So much for television. As for the trade, the company RSF realizes an unhoped-for commercial operation by selling anti-Chinese T-shirts which will end up bringing in, she trumpets, a million euros.

The Olympic flame goes through Paris, brandished by well supervised athletes. When it is the turn of a young paralyzed Chinese woman, Jin Jing, to carry it in her wheelchair, some people throw themselves on her to take it away. Jostled, she will defend her victoriously. The images of this scene will make the turn of the world. They will be diffused in loop by the Chinese televisions. In Paris, the Chinese officials, ulcerated, decide to interrupt the course.

In France, one cannot imagine the importance of the Chinese word *mianzi*, which means "face", "social identity"; to lack *mianzi* is to lose face, to suffer an affront. This is how the Chinese perceived the events surrounding the Olympic flame in Paris.

With this success, RSF increases the pressure on President Nicolas Sarkozy to boycott the opening ceremony of the Games and that France is officially absent. The NGO makes realize a poll which shows that the majority of the French is at present favorable to the boycott. The president Sarkozy dithers, reserves his decision, hears unofficial Chinese voices which finish by saying: "He comes if he wants, but he will not be welcome. Finally, he flew on August 8 for a quick round trip. Twenty hours of travel, ten hours on site, not even a night. It was, ironically enough, "the sprint of Speedy Sarko in Beijing"[105].

During the parade of athletes, the enthusiastic crowd does not spare its applause. Except for the French who will be whistled.

Jean-Pierre Raffarin, former Prime Minister, flew to Beijing a few days later, in a difficult context where Chinese public opinion, traditionally favorable to France since General de Gaulle spoke out in favor of the admission of mainland China to the UN (instead of Formosa), showed a new hostility. In Beijing, the French embassy advised French citizens to be discreet and cautious. Demonstrations took place in front of French stores.

Christian Poncelet, President of the Senate and therefore the second most important person of the State, will also be sent to Beijing. He is carrying words of appeasement, a letter of sympathy from President Sarkozy. He wants to visit Jin Jing, the athlete who was attacked in Paris.

A few months later, in December 2008, Nicolas Sarkozy met the Dalai Lama in Gdansk, in the north of Poland, "as president of the Council of Europe"[106].

France, which no more than any other country in the world recognizes the existence of Tibet as a state, is exhausting itself in a waltz

105. "Le sprint de speedy Sarko à Pékin", *20 minutes*, 5 August 2008.
106. AFP, December 6, 2008.

of hesitation that would not be appropriate if politicians had true information on the Dalai Lama's plans, on the use he is making and would make of his temporal power, all of which they should distance themselves from if they value their image as democrats attached to our Constitution. As for the French people, whose approval of the separation of Church and State is no longer to be demonstrated, they would not be able to support, as soon as they are informed, maneuvers of all kinds that would lead to the establishment of a theocracy. He is also surprised that the Western supporters of the Dalai Lama refrain from defending the slightest social demand for Tibetans, a field in which there is still much to be done. But to speak about it would oblige to do the same under our windows.

Neither will he appreciate the counterproductive gesticulations that do not advance the issues raised one iota, that err on the side of selectivity by reserving exclusive hatred for one of the one hundred and fifty or more countries that operate with a system that we in France would not want, gesticulations that curiously spare a superpower that regularly carries terror, torture, destruction, massacres in territories far from its borders, within which a *soft* electoral alternation hums, ensured by the disinterest of an immense mass of non-voters, by the colossal sums necessary to whoever wants to be a candidate for an election, the whole constituting a democratic sauce which ensures the perenniality of its credo: *bizness is bizness.*

XI
The NGO and the CIA dollars

Reporters Without Borders has organized anti-Chinese demonstrations on the basis of a bias permanently displayed on its website. For example, it gives the official list of Asian countries recognized by international bodies, adding, on its own initiative, Tibet. This is a way for RSF to officially grant this Chinese region an independence that is not recognized by the UN and which the Dalai Lama says he no longer wants.

Was RSF seeking in 2008 to promote greater freedom in Tibet? If so, everyone would agree, if not with its methods, at least with its objectives. Was it fighting for Tibetan media? No. Rather, an examination of its activities and statements shows that RSF has long been part of an international political effort to separate Tibet from China.

Already in 2001, she participated, with the activists of the organization France-Tibet, which advocates the independence of Tibet, in an attempt to question the Chinese president Hu Jintao at his exit from the French Institute of International Relations. Here is what we read on the France-Tibet website on November 5, 2001: "We were six members of Reporters Without Borders, including Robert Ménard, the secretary general, and three activists from France-Tibet [...] Brandishing Tibetan flags, while chanting 'Democracy in China!

Freedom in Tibet!", our friends from RSF threw leaflets in the direction of the delegation calling for the release of the Tibetan Ngawang Choephel and other political prisoners.

RSF has long been much more advanced than NGOs whose role it is to deal with these specific issues, such as Amnesty International. On March 25, 2008, the French coordinator of this NGO for China declared that she was "against all boycotts, including the boycott of opening ceremonies by politicians".

The Dalai Lama says the same thing. But RSF goes ahead, invested with a sacred mission that delights its sponsors across the Atlantic.

On April 3, 2008, according to Tibet-Info: "Every time the flame crosses a city, we will be there to say 'don't forget the reality of Tibet, don't forget the reality of China,'" said R. Menard. Still two countries.

On April 6, 2008, we read on the website of RSF: "Reporters Without Borders calls on all Parisians to go from noon to the foot of the Eiffel Tower, wearing a T-shirt representing the Olympic rings in the form of handcuffs or black to demonstrate for human rights in China and Tibet.

In China AND in Tibet! We can see that the appeal still states that there are two distinct countries and that the organization that claims to defend journalists is extending its action to "human rights" in general and to the delimitation of the borders of an Asian country in particular, roles usually assigned to others.

George W. Bush is an expert on human rights, as he has shown in Afghanistan and Iraq. This is perhaps why, on April 8, 2008, in a courteous letter to him, RSF asked him not to attend the opening ceremony of the Games in Beijing. Robert Ménard will avoid thereafter, even in his book published in October 2008, to focus more on the American president.

On June 25, 2008, RSF urged the International Olympic Committee to demand an apology from China for remarks made in Lhasa by Chinese officials, one of whom had called for "crushing the plots of the Dalai Lama's clique and hostile foreign forces seeking to ruin the

Beijing Olympics"[107]. Here we see Menard slipping even further by forgetting his primary mission. He now behaves like an ambassador in charge of defending the Dalai Lama in Europe.

The opening ceremony went off without a hitch for the organizers and for the athletes from all over the world (except ours), with the magnificence that we know. At RSF, we are bitter. The Chinese people have made a spectacular turnaround with respect to France, but the Chinese authorities are keeping their cool. Shouldn't RSF be more aggressive with the French government? Here's what Ménard writes: "Nicolas Sarkozy was in the gallery on August 8 in Beijing, seated alongside a lineup of great democrats: the presidents of Vietnam, Pakistan, Russia... George Bush too."[108] Bush, added at the end, as if with regret, as an obligatory "repentance". Ménard and RSF will say nothing more. Others will not benefit from such leniency. The Reuters agency headlines a dispatch of August 4, 2008: *Robert Ménard is very angry*:

"By sparing China, Nicolas Sarkozy is participating in a 'coalition of cowards' which includes the president of the International Olympic Committee (IOC) Jacques Rogge," says the secretary general of Reporters Without Borders.

One notices that in the "coalition of cowards" one finds the French president (for whom Ménard says he voted during the presidential elections), but not the then occupant of the White House, the executioner of Iraq (where more than two hundred journalists and assimilated have fallen) and of Afghanistan, chief torturer of Guantanamo.

In his book, the activist complains: "If you type on Google: 'Robert Menard + CIA', the search site offers you... one hundred and fourteen thousand links."[109] Checked, the figure is lower, but very high nevertheless.

We will understand why.

---

107. Statement by Zhang Qingli in Lhasa in front of the Potala on June 21, 2008. Reported by the AFP on June 26, 2008.
108. Ménard (Robert), *op. cit.*, p. 20.
109. *Ibid.*, p. 127.

The National Endowment for Democracy (NED), which we have said subsidizes the Dalai Lama, also subsidizes Reporters Without Borders, which has also received money from the Taiwanese Foundation for Democracy. Robert Ménard, RSF's secretary general at the time, went to Taiwan on January 28, 2007 to receive a check for one hundred thousand dollars from President Chen Shui-bian, acting on behalf of this foundation, which is active in China.

When I was writing my book on RSF[110], I asked Robert Ménard to give me a copy of the contract between him and the NED. I was unable to obtain it. On the other hand, I read directly, on the US government website, a document where the NED explains to the beneficiary NGOs what they commit to. The NGO must state the precise objectives to be reached in the country of implementation of its project. For example, to improve the leadership skills of activists and to build the organizational capacity of local associations. It must provide tangible evidence of change or results achieved: election results, votes on laws, court records, legislative or judicial documents, media reports, etc. These obligations explain RSF's policy against certain countries.

But, says the NED, it must not engage in activities whose purpose is to influence US public policy. This prohibition makes it almost impossible for RSF to condemn or stop the assassinations of journalists in Yugoslavia, and later in Iraq or Afghanistan when the American army is involved. Similarly, RSF cannot condemn the presence of Bush at the opening ceremony of the Olympic Games, as it has condemned the presence of other heads of state.

Finally, if one assumes that the United States, worried about the rise of a great power and anxious to remain masters of a unipolar world, sees in the financing of the Dalai-Lamist separatist movement a means of weakening China, and even of setting foot (and military bases) on the "Roof of the World", it is not surprising to see RSF deploying a feverish activity on this same site.

---

110. Vivas (Maxime), *op. cit.*

On Friday, September 26, 2008, Robert Ménard created a surprise by announcing that he was leaving RSF on the following Tuesday "because he wanted to do something else". By way of wanting to do something else, he went around in circles for a while, publicly considered various hypotheses and ended up selling himself to Qatar, a polygamous, misogynistic Arab dictatorship, where foreign workers are treated like the serfs of Tibet under the Dalai Lamas (the United Nations Special Rapporteur on Trafficking in Persons, especially women and children, has expressed concern about immigrant workers being "trafficked," where flogging is a legal punishment, where the death penalty is in effect, where the press is forbidden to criticize the ruling royal family, and where laws are made not by the elected representatives of the people, but by Sharia law).

Today, he rants on a private television channel where, according to an article in a major French weekly, he "flouts" human rights "every morning on his show by humiliating and insulting his guests"[111].

111. Besson (Patrick), "L'interview selon Robert Ménard", *Le Point*, 25 November 2010.

XII
The Dalai Lama's governing program

"We have recently initiated changes that will later democratize and strengthen our administration in exile."[112]

How to rally international opinion to Dalai Lamaism while leaving a dictatorial constitution attached to the branch of Buddhism represented by His Holiness? It is so impossible that the Dalai Lama will use the word *democracy* abundantly and that he will pronounce speeches showing his will to wipe out the past. Unfortunately, when we study his texts and see how he deals with his opponents (Shugden), it appears that the old demons are still there, lurking in the wings, waiting for better days.

In his speech to the European Parliament in Strasbourg on October 24, 2001, the Dalai Lama explained democracy: "This year we have made another great step forward in the process of democratization by having the chairman of the Tibetan Cabinet elected by universal suffrage. But he immediately adds that this parliament and the deputies will be limited to "running the day-to-day business...", with the main role still vested in him: "However, I consider it a moral

112. Speech by the Dalai Lama, "Buddhism and Democracy," Washington D.C., April 1993.

duty to the six million Tibetans, to continue to work on the Tibetan issue with the Chinese leadership and to act as the free voice of the Tibetans until we have reached a solution."

For my still skeptical reader, here are excerpts from the charter (constitutionally binding program) of government drawn up by the Dalai Lama from Dharamsala. It should be noted here that the content of this document is so unacceptable and has had such a negative impact that the Dalai Lama now claims that it is only valid for the period of exile and will not be applied in Tibet. Strangely enough, it has disappeared from websites supporting the Dalai Lama.

Article 3 states the "nature of Tibetan politics": "The future Tibetan politics shall respect the principle of non-violence and shall strive to be a free welfare state whose politics shall be guided by the Dharma."

The *dharma*, that is to say a religious law, which takes precedence over the civil law, which would make us cry out in France.

In Article 36, it is the conception of legislative power that is developed: "All legislative power and authority reside in the Tibetan Assembly. The decisions of the Assembly require the approval of His Holiness the Dalai Lama to become law. The Assembly has all the power... if His Holiness wants it! As Article 19, on executive power, testifies:

"The executive power of the Tibetan administration is vested in His Holiness the Dalai Lama, and shall be exercised by him, either directly or through officers subordinate to him, in accordance with the provisions of this Charter. In particular, His Holiness the Dalai Lama is empowered to execute the following powers as the head of the leadership of the Tibetan people:

(a) approve and promulgate bills and regulations prescribed by the Tibetan Assembly.

(b) enact laws and ordinances that have the force of law.

(c) confer honors and awards of merit.

(d) to convene, adjourn, postpone and extend the Tibetan Assembly.

(e) send messages and addresses to the Tibetan Assembly whenever necessary.

(f) suspend or dissolve the Tibetan Assembly.

(g) dissolve the Kashag (government) or remove a Kalon (minister).

(h) declare an emergency and call special meetings of great importance.

(j) authorize referendums in cases involving major outstanding issues in accordance with this Charter."

This is clear: neither leader nor involved in "democratic" government, but above the common people and institutions, self-proclaimed spokesman, living god, and supreme guide.

The Charter ends with a "special resolution", passed in 1991, which reads: "His Holiness the Dalai Lama, the supreme leader of the Tibetan people, has offered the ideals of democracy to the Tibetan people, even if they have not felt the need for these ideals. All Tibetans, in Tibet and in exile, are and remain deeply grateful to His Holiness the Dalai Lama, and recommit ourselves to establish our faith and allegiance to the leadership of His Holiness the Dalai Lama, and to pray fervently that he may remain with us forever as our supreme spiritual and temporal leader."

XIII
Long live secularism and democracy, here and elsewhere!

"The social life of this vast and arid country [...] resembles that of our Middle Ages. The sovereignty of the clergy is strongly established. The absolute monarch of the country is the great religious leader, a pontiff held to be superhuman."[113]

If there is one strong value that unites the French, it is that of secularism, the separation of Church and State. The law of December 9, 1905 ensures this with its principles of reciprocal non-interference: religions must not have any influence on politics and vice versa. Through the secularization of the State, freedom of belief and worship is guaranteed and beliefs are equal among themselves.

In our country, the implementation of the principle of secularism, that is to say of a new concept of coexistence between the civil and the religious, could not be done without calling into question the exorbitant prerogatives of the Church, fruits of its past omnipotence, even of a political-ideological totalitarianism (auto-da-fés, blacklisting, Inquisition, burning at the stake, Saint Bartholomew's

113. David-Néel (Alexandra), *Mercure de France*, June [1,] 1920.

Day...). In other words, the birth of secularism was accompanied by the disappearance of certain religious privileges. It was a fight in which the Republic wanted to see an extension of freedoms, and the Church a persecution.

Our country respects all religions and all believers. It is not atheist, it is obliged by law to protect believers against all discrimination, but secular law takes precedence over religious precepts. The Constitution cannot take a back seat to "sacred" texts.

A century after the adoption of the 1905 law, few French people advocate restoring to the Catholic religion its former privileges. The almost unanimous opinion is that it should stay away from political, judicial and legislative power. No religion could interfere in the affairs of state, control the government or exercise any political function.

However, there remains a (very) small minority of French people, affected by a logic that is not very Cartesian, which makes them cherish secularism here and dream of the creation of a distant state that would abolish it as a preamble to the dismemberment of the country, which they would certainly not want at home (our imprisoned independentists will understand me).

This principle of secularism is inapplicable in a country in which a man would be invested, according to his religion, with spiritual and temporal power by divine privilege resulting from the miracle of his birth.

In other words, it is not enough for the aging Dalai Lama, defeated in his struggle to rule Tibet, to say today, a little late, from Dharamsala: let me return as a "simple monk", I renounce all powers (not quite, since he intends to retain "moral and religious authority"). There is no point in his calling for a "free, modern, secular, democratic Tibet that respects the constitution of China" if, at the same time, he organizes a theocratic government in exile with a Minister of Religion and Culture, a Department of Religious Affairs, and forty-three deputies, two of whom represent each of the four schools of Buddhism and two the pre-Buddhist religion.

The *Official Translation of the Guidelines for Future Tibet's Polity and Basic* Features *of Its Constitution, Which His Holiness Issued on* 26 February 1992, announces that since education is the key to development special attention will be given to formulating a *sound* educational policy with all necessary assistance to schools, universities, institutes of science, technology and other professional training.

What kind of education? Who will provide it in these schools that did not exist during the time of the Dalai Lamas' absolute power and that could only come into being when he fled to India? The organization of schools in the Tibetan community in exile, with obligatory prayers and a portrait of the Dalai Lama in every classroom, raises fears of a great leap backwards in the evolution of education in Tibet.

His contradictions, his incessant reversals over the course of the days, are discrediting his word. For him to be believed, stronger and more contractualized commitments are needed, the dissolution of his "government" where half (three out of six) of the members of the cabinet are from his family and where other relatives still occupy more or less important functions in Parliament and in bodies with foreign relations. What is needed, no doubt, is an *aggiornamento* of the fossilized dogma of the branch of Buddhism he represents, bringing it into line with the 21st century, renouncing intervention in public teaching, and taking a critical inventory of what Tibet was like under thirteen Dalai Lamas, and what it was like under his own reign. It requires the acceptance of the data and progress that indelibly mark modern societies where power emanates (at least in theory) from the people and not from a deity. It is necessary to refuse everything that is likely to induce cultural, economic, political and social stagnation. It is necessary to admit publicly and without reserve that education is a benefit. Shouldn't it be necessary, by a secular charter, still unwritten after so much time of exile and discovery of other worlds, to renounce the expulsion of the populations originating from one of the fifty-five other ethnic groups which populate China, to guarantee the non-return to the fusion of powers for a religious and idle fraction? To pronounce for the right to mixed marriages (Tibetans and other ethnic groups), to accept the existence of other religions and the right to practice none?

Recent statements by the Dalai Lama have disoriented those who saw in him an ocean of wisdom. If the Dalai Lama declares himself in favor of condoms and contraceptive methods, when questioned about homosexuality by the weekly magazine *Le Point* on March 23, 2001, he replies:

"This is part of what we Buddhists call 'sexual misconduct'. The sexual organs were created for reproduction between the male and female elements and anything that deviates from this is not acceptable from a Buddhist point of view [he lists fingers]: between a man and a man, a woman and another woman, in the mouth, the anus, or even using the hand [he mimes the gesture of masturbation]."[114] Faced with the emotion aroused by this statement, he will later instruct his spokesmen to qualify it by explaining that Buddhism is not homophobic.

While it is permissible to change one's mind and reshape ukases and claims over decades, years, or even days, the piling up of contradictory discourses is surprising and worrying.

For, at the same time as he affirms that he accepts today all that he did not want yesterday and which led him to the insurrection, and then to half a century of anti-Chinese diplomatic guerrilla warfare throughout the world, he perpetuates from India a "Tibetan government in exile", It produces documents and speeches which are in line with past requirements, it does not carry out any inventory, it marks repeated reserves on the virtues of the instruction, it intervenes to exclude from the Tibetan community in exile those which it designates as heretics, criminals, agents of the Chinese devil. Finally, he called his proposal for independence the "Middle Way" and drew up a "Charter of Government" which did so little to conceal its theocratic

114. Gautier (François), " Sexe, morale et vache folle : le dalaï-lama parle ", *Le Point*, 23 mars 2001, http://www.lepoint.fr/archives/article.php/69035

essence that he had to say that it applied only to his "kingdom" of Dharamsala and that it would not be applied in Tibet.

"The Dalai Lama does not have the dubious ambition of restoring an outdated and ancient regime"[115], he is told by his entourage. But what outdated and ancient practices or mores is he talking about exactly? He has never described them in detail. Does the regime he does not want to restore suffer only from being too old? From nothing else? So the time has not yet come for repentance and distancing oneself from what was the Tibet of the Dalai Lamas. This silence is deafening. It leaves the door open to all fanatical and liberticidal outbreaks.

"As much as we adopt modern lifestyles in exile, we cherish and preserve our identity and culture and thereby sustain the hopes of millions of our compatriots.[116] Are we to understand that modern ways of life would be abandoned upon his hypothetical return to Tibet? Does the preservation of identity allow intermarriage with Chinese of other ethnicities and foreigners, or does it lead to the creed of "pure race"? Does the culture to be preserved extend to past social and political mores?

The Dalai Lama returning to Lhasa would be like the old wolf of ancient tales entering the sheepfold of the 21st century, the implicit promise of a return to square one, that of the years before 1959, not by the identical reappearance of the feudal state which no Tibetan would want, but by the possibility that he would have, from his immense palace of the Potala, to call for a coup de force and for the help of the foreigner for the re-establishment, on an immense region, of his temporal power, of certain privileges and of the old prejudices of Buddhism. I am convinced that this will happen, opening a world crisis, triggering bloody troubles, at the end of which China will be weakened and bruised, but Tibet will be ravaged and Buddhism

---

115. "Organization of the Tibetan Community in Exile. The Tibetan Government in Exile," September 10, 2009, http://www.savetibet.fr/2009/09/organisation-de-la-communaute-tibetaine-en-exil-le-gouvernement-tibetain-en-exil/.
116. Dalai Lama, Nobel Peace Prize acceptance speech, December 10, 1989.

will be discredited, held as a suspicious and harmful political theory, enemy of the "glorious fatherland". This is the common fate of religions that invest themselves with temporal power. They end up being victims of it. "Dominant, they compromise their spiritual dimension; dominated, they suffer the discrimination that comes from the existence of an official creed."[117]

It is fashionable in French hipsters to accept the price to be paid by others, according to the principle that those who push are not those who fall.

Some people, including myself, take a stand for the respect of life, for the right of Buddhists to practice a religion which, by not becoming a political Trojan horse, would not put itself in a position to be fought. "But the Tibetan religion, suspected - not without reason - of having a link with political dissidence and "separatism", remains under close surveillance."[118]

We know that, for its part, the Muslim religion, a component of which is suspected of links with terrorism, is the object of particular vigilance in Atlanticist countries, sometimes of persecution, often of press campaigns. The recent past has taught us how citizens of different countries of the world, just because they are Muslims, have been kidnapped by the CIA, caged, humiliated, tortured, driven mad, even murdered in the prison of Guantanamo. The autonomous region of Xinjiang, populated by Uyghurs of the Muslim faith, worked on its borders by Pakistani and Afghan fundamentalists, poses a problem in China. The NED is developing four intervention programs for this region.

Wouldn't all this prove, if it were still necessary, that belief and governance do not benefit from being mixed, both losing serenity and credit?

---

117. Pena-Ruiz (Henri), *Qu'est-ce que laïcité?* Paris, Gallimard, 2003.
118. Report of the interparliamentary friendship group of the Senate, October 17, 2007.

Who could be against the right of all Chinese, in Tibet and elsewhere, to live in peace, not in an institutional status quo that would accommodate the state of democracy in China, but by encouraging everything that could accelerate its progress (which exists), by prohibiting any attitude that would encourage Beijing to take a step backwards, which has engraved in Western consciousness a negative image of China, an image that is not a caricature due to its external enemies, but which corresponds to what it was, to what it still remains in certain aspects and to the inability of our media to see others?

If lovers of Tibet and its culture, and even of Buddhism, work for an ever better harmonization of relations between the central government and this sensitive region, if they push for an accelerated democratization of China, if they do not tolerate the press campaigns that stir up hatred based on lies that end up in useless violence, they will have contributed to the advent of a better world without having at any time been obliged to subscribe to the political, economic, judicial, social, and media systems of the Middle Kingdom.

As we can see, this book, which lacks empathy for the Dalai Lama as a devious political leader, is not a pamphlet against Buddhism: it deplores its misuse for purposes that we would be surprised (and sorry) to learn are enshrined in immutable sacred texts.

Was it a question here of praising China and declaring today's Tibet a paradise? One will look in vain for the pages where I fell into this trap. I like to quote Jean-Luc Mélenchon: "I am not a Chinese communist. I will never be one. But I do not agree with the demonstrations in favor of the boycott of the Olympic Games. I do not agree with the operation of Robert Menard against the Olympic Games in Beijing. I do not agree with the rewriting of the history of China to which this whole operation gives rise. I do not share at all the blissful enthusiasm for the Dalai Lama nor for the regime he embodies."[119]

119. See Jean-Luc Mélenchon's blog, http://www.jean-luc-melenchon.fr/2008/04/07/je-ne-suis-pas-daccord-avec-le-boycott-des-jeux-de-pekin-et-la-propagande-anti-chinoise/, April 7, 2008.

In short, in writing this book, I had no other aim than to contribute to the free exercise of Buddhism, to civil peace, to democratic progress and to the material and intellectual development of Tibet, which has been held in alienation, stagnation and unhappiness for too long by political and religious fanaticism.

For the reasons stated, China will not give up the autonomous region of Tibet, Tibet of which the Dalai Lama, his followers and sponsors are the evil geniuses.

Bibliography

Dalai Lama:

Memoirs of the Dalai Lama. My land and my people, Paris, John Didier, 1963.

Freedom for Tibet. Message of peace and tolerance, Paris, L'Arganier, 2008.

Nobel Peace Prize acceptance speech, December 10, 1989.

Charter of Government of Tibetans in Exile, June 14, 1991.

Official Translation of the Guidelines for Future Tibet's Polity and Basic Features of Its Constitution, Which His Holiness Issued on 26 February 1992.

Speech "Buddhism and Democracy", Washington D.C., April 1993.

Speech at the European Parliament in Strasbourg, 24 October 2001.

Press conference in Strasbourg, 24 October 2001.

Statement at the forty-ninth anniversary of the Tibetan National Uprising Day in Dharamsala, March 10, 2008.

Other :

ARON (Raymond), *Memoirs*, Paris, Robert Laffont, 2003.

DAVID-NÉEL (Alexandra), *Grand Tibet et vaste Chine*, Paris, Omnibus, 1996.

MÉNARD (Robert), *Des libertés et autres chinoiseries*, Paris, Robert Laffont, 2008.

NICOL (Mike), *Inspirations and words of the Dalai Lama*, Acropole, Paris, 2008.

VIVAS (Maxime), *La Face cachée de Reporters sans frontières. De la CIA aux faucons du Pentagone*, Paris, Aden, 2007.

Report of the Franco-Tibetan friendship group of the Senate*, June 14, 2006.*

Report of the interparliamentary friendship group of the Senate, *17 October 2007.*

France 24, report of August 9, 2008.

National Endowment for Democracy, website, January 2011.

International Centre for Prison Studies, King's College, London.

As well as :

Reporters Without Borders, Amnesty International, France-Tibet, Tibet-Info, AFP, *Der Spiegel*, *Libération*, France Culture, *Le Point*, *Los Angeles Times*, *Le Monde diplomatique*, *Washington Post*, *New York Times*.

TABLE OF CONTENTS

www.ingramcontent.com/pod-product-compliance
Ingram Content Group UK Ltd.
Pitfield, Milton Keynes, MK11 3LW, UK
UKHW022012260726
13994UKWH00006B/2436